NOEL

*Bringing Your God-Designed
Destiny to Life*

Micah Sutton

NOEL: Bringing Your God-Designed Destiny to Life

Micah Sutton

Published by:
Micah Sutton

ISBN-10: 0578413779

ISBN-13: 978-0-578-41377-8

Printed in the United States of America

Dedicated to those who have taught me to dream, lead, and do. My parents Bobby and Karen Sutton taught me to believe God could do anything. My grandfather, Alfred Stephens (A.K.A Pawpaw) believed I could do almost anything. My wife Kristy has walked with me as we've tried to do everything. For each of these incredible people in my life I am grateful.

Contents

Foreword

I'm sitting in a hotel room in Washington, DC and I've just read NOEL for the first time. Something has leapt in my heart tonight as I have followed the excellent craftsmanship of words explaining the process of birthing a destiny. The journey the author has designed for the reader is one that seems familiar, yet the unexpected continually pokes its head into your consciousness as nuggets of divine truth are unexpectedly dropped like handfuls on purpose. Prepare to smile, nod and affirm truth as you see it uncovered, but also prepare yourself to be surprised, accosted and challenged with truths you didn't expect.

I've known Micah Sutton for many years and always expect greatness from him. I've seen him on his mountaintops, and I've walked with him through some dark valleys. I've been close to him and Kristy as well as their sons, so with longevity comes familiarity and that's why Noel was an unexpected surprise, the sleeper manuscript that has manifest destiny slumbering deep within its pages waiting to be opened to spring to life and maturation within each of us. Like an experienced builder of one of life's greatest experiences, Micah lays the courses of brick constantly and consistently through chapters, building a great wall of understanding the *"how"* behind the *"what."* Each reader will be challenged to move forward in the maturation process... now, please hand me another brick, I want to get on with what God has designed for me.

Brett Jones, Senior Pastor,
Grace Church, Houston, TX

CHAPTER 1

Be It Unto Me

Christmas. There isn't any other word in the English language that sparks excitement in young children and adults alike. It has been the subject of countless books, songs, and movies. The Christmas season is a special, magical time of year in which anything can happen.

When I was growing up, I always looked forward to Christmas. When the first day of December came around, my anticipation would begin to rise. At night, images of the incredible gifts I would receive began to make their way into my dreams. During the day, visions of the heroic deeds that I would accomplish filled my heart and mind. I could see myself fighting off the enemy with my new BB gun. I imagined the glory I would bring to God and the feeling of my mother's admiration as I played the new instrument I was sure to get for Christmas.

We often spent the holidays at my grandparents' home in Baton Rouge, Louisiana, where aunts and uncles and cousins would gather by the dozens. It was always a wonderful time. Because there were preparations to be made, mom and dad would tell us of the trip several weeks in advance. From that point forward, I could hardly keep still. The anticipation of seeing everyone and having Christmas with the whole family was almost too much to bear.

In those days, the idea of receiving gifts was exciting. I can remember the year that all changed for me. It was 1999. That was the year my wife, Kristy, and I had our first son. He was born in July and was six months old that first Christmas. We had just moved to California, we were broke, and we were uncertain about life in general. I don't believe Kristy and I bought gifts for each other at all that year, but that little six-month-old boy named Talon, he got gifts. I couldn't wait to give them to him. I could not wait to see his face as he opened them. They weren't much, but they were being given to our son. He really didn't even care about the presents at all. In fact, the paper was much more fascinating to him than the gift. This Christmas was still joyous and full of anticipation, but for a different reason. That is what giving birth will do.

As a Christian, Christmas is a time for me to celebrate the birth of my savior, Jesus Christ. I love the songs referring to his birth: *"Joy to the world! The Lord has come," "Go, tell it on the mountain. Over the hills and everywhere," "Away in a manger, no crib for a bed."* All these songs spark the imagination as they bring to mind the night the Christ child was brought into this world. The Savior was born, Jesus had arrived. One song, however, has always been a favorite – The First Noel. I've always loved it, but I've not always understood it.

The song is obviously telling the story of Christ's birth. I'm not confused by that at all, but when the beautiful melody leads us into saying, *"Noel, Noel, Noel, Noel; Born is the King of Israel,"* that is where my confusion lay. The song is telling this beautiful story of the Christ child born and then breaks into this repeated refrain of Noel. The song is so beautiful that I would sing it with gusto, but it wasn't until Christmas of 2010 that I understood the incredible reality being proclaimed by the song.

Noel is French for *"the Christmas season"* and goes back much farther than the 14th century. It was derived from the Latin word for *"birth."* Imagine singing the word *"birth"* repeatedly instead of Noel. Go ahead, try it. It just doesn't have the same ring to it. However, birth is what the Christmas season is all about. The first Christmas was the birth of the Savior of the world. It has become a time of celebrating with friends and family, giving gifts to others, and the general recognition of the Christ child. But that's not how Christmas started. It began in a little town called Nazareth with a conversation between an angel named Gabriel and a young Jewish girl by the name of Mary.

A Girl with a Destiny

The story goes like this: Mary was living her life just like many other young ladies of her time. We know that she was looking forward to being married to her fiancé, Joseph, and was probably preparing to be a good wife. We don't know a lot about Mary, but we do know that Joseph was a carpenter. This would have placed him in the artisan class of society. He was not a peasant, but he was not high class at all. Since marriage arrangements usually involved people of similar station, Mary probably lived a modest lifestyle. She wasn't poor but would have likely been close.

I don't know exactly how it happened. The pictures depicting this moment show many different variations, but we don't know for sure. Some show a frightened young lady with a laundry basket of woven straw laying askew at her feet while a glowing angel holds out his hand to her. Others show Mary sitting in her bed as if woken from a night's sleep. Still others reveal a woman bowing herself to the ground as the angel speaks. I don't know exactly what it looked like, but I do know what was said.

Gabriel said to Mary, *"Rejoice, highly favored one, the Lord is with you; blessed are you among women!"* What an introduction. I love how understated the scripture often is. After this out-of-this-world introduction, the Bible says that when Mary saw him, *"she was troubled at his saying, and considered what manner of greeting this was."* This was the Bible's way of saying that Mary was totally freaked out. Here she was, just going about her day, when an angel appeared out of nowhere and started declaring she should rejoice, that she was favored, and she was blessed among women. For a woman of her status in life, his words may have been hard to believe even with a normal presentation. With this type of introduction, her response was anything but calm and reserved.

Gabriel, seeing her confusion tried to calm her down by saying, *"Don't be afraid. Mary, for you have found favor with God"*[1]. He appeared out of nowhere declaring great blessings, and now he even knows her name! This angel is too much! This alone would have been worthy of including in the scripture, but this angel was just getting started. Gabriel starts telling her that she would bring forth a son. She was going to call him Jesus. He was going to be great and be the Son of God. He would have a kingdom that descended from the throne of David. Not only was all of this going to be true, but the kingdom that her son would rule over would have no end. It would last forever.

When God places a vision, a dream, into your life, it is rarely small. It will almost never seem possible. It will always provoke a sense of destiny.

It is interesting that when God places a vision, a dream, into your life, it is rarely small. It will almost never seem possible. It will always provoke a sense of destiny. As the angel declared these amazing things, Mary listened. It would have been easy for her to walk away. It would have made sense if she simply stepped out of the room and forgot everything she had seen or heard. In anyone's world this would have been overwhelming. Mary could have walked away, but she didn't. Mary asked a question.

To paraphrase, *"I hear what you are saying, angel. I understand the everlasting kingdom, the throne of David, the favor with God, and even the son of the Highest, but I have one little bitty question. You said I was going to have a son. How is that going to happen since I'm a virgin and I'm not getting married anytime soon?"* This is a huge question. The angel Gabriel had just outlined Mary's destiny. He had revealed her purpose with clarity that few have ever experienced. Mary wanted to know how this process was going to begin. What was going to happen that would move her from the promise to the fulfillment of what God had designed her to do?

Everyone arrives at this question when they realize they too have a destiny ordained by God. The day you realize that God has a plan for your life, you begin asking two questions: What is my destiny, and how will it come to pass?

Your Destiny Is Calling

Here is the thing about a God-designed destiny: It rarely follows natural methods or normal pathways. When God desired to bring Israel out of slavery in Egypt, He walked them through the bottom of the Red Sea. Yeah, He had to part the water so they would not drown, but that's how He chose to do it. When God decided that Israel would defeat Jericho in battle, He told them to walk around the city silently for six days and on the seventh day...shout. There were a few more instructions, but none of them made Israel's victory any more *"normal."* Now, God is going to introduce His Son, the Savior, into the world, and His methodology was again – abnormal. It wasn't natural, but then again, nothing about God is natural. Nothing about God qualifies as *"normal"* to humanity.

You are called by God for a particular purpose.

This book is for people to understand that there is a future designed for you. Just as Mary was called by God to fulfill a particular purpose, you are called by God for a particular purpose. There is something that God has specifically designed you for, a job to complete, a destiny to fulfill. It may not be the angel Gabriel who stands before you in your room. There may be no declaration as specific as Mary's. There will, however, be a moment when what God has called you to do will become clear. A moment when your mind will be captivated by a particular idea. That idea will float across your mind and crystalize, growing sharper by the moment. It will be then that your spirit will respond. The idea may seem crazy, it may fall entirely outside of what is normal or usual, but something about it calls to you, and it won't let you go. Your destiny is calling.

Time to Choose

It is at that moment when destiny becomes clear that a choice must be made. A choice to either follow God's plan or walk away from the clear call. What would've happened if Mary had chosen to step out of the room as the angel was speaking? Would we know her name at all? Would she have been included in the stories of those who might have been something great in the kingdom of God? We don't know the answer to these questions because Mary chose to step into the destiny God had planned for her.

Think about it this way: God was asking Mary to have a child that was miraculously seeded into her womb. That was asking a lot already. Add to that the fact that she was already engaged to this guy Joseph. At best, Mary was probably going to lose her fiancé and at worst, she might lose her life. They were still stoning people in those days, and pregnancy outside of marriage wasn't looked upon favorably. Saying that it was God's baby was not going to make things any better.

When Gabriel spoke God's plan to Mary, she had a question. She asked, *"How is this going to happen since I've not slept with a man."* Notice that Mary did not dismiss the idea. She did not say, *"This is impossible."* She brought up the obvious issue. She asked, and Gabriel answered. I'm not certain that Gabriel's answer made it any clearer for Mary, but she did learn that this birth was going to be anything but natural or normal.

Gabriel said, *"The Holy Spirit will cover you and impregnate you."* And if what he said wasn't incredible enough already, Gabriel continued, *"...and that Holy One that you give birth to will be called the Son of God."* Mary must have been standing there in utter disbelief. Then Gabriel went on to say that she would give birth to a son who would save his people.

At this time, Israel had languished under Roman rule for many years. They were not in control of their own land or their own destiny and they wanted to be. There were many rumblings of leaders planning to rise up and save the people from Rome's rule. By this time, several had tried to liberate Israel, but none had been successful. The ancient prophets foretold of a savior who would be born among the people. Mary could have easily thought that Gabriel was telling her that her son would be that savior. It was far-fetched to think that she would be the mother of that great leader, but at least it was within some realm of possibility.

Learning that this child would be the Son of God - that took things to a whole new level, a level Mary was not prepared to think about. When Gabriel shared this new bit of information with Mary, she didn't even ask a question. Why not? I believe the answer is simple: What do you say to that?

Here we have a heavenly messenger, an incredible promise, a divine destiny, and a miraculous process that are all staring an underprivileged, young Jewish lady in the eye. Gabriel was waiting for a response.

In my mind, I imagine the scene unfolding kind of like this: Gabriel is looking at Mary with intensity and excitement. He has just announced that she had been chosen to give birth to the Savior of mankind.

Mary is looking back at Gabriel as long seconds pass. Her mind is racing. What would this experience be like? What would it mean to be pregnant? What would it feel like to get pregnant? Getting pregnant by God was both a bonus and a huge question mark. How would Joseph respond? Would she lose him? What would her parents say? What would the community say? What would it be like raising a baby - not to mention God's baby? It is not so much that she has no questions, it is just there are so many that she has no idea where to even begin.

I don't know exactly what this looked like, but I do know that at some point Mary had to conclude that answering all of these questions may not be possible at this time. She had to accept that she might lose Joseph, the community around her may not understand, and she would experience much pain. She eventually understood each of those things, but the joy that was set before her outweighed the pain that she would feel in giving birth to the plan God had for her life.

Mary opened her mouth and uttered the words that would change the world forever. *"Then Mary said, 'Behold the maidservant of the Lord! Let it be to me according to your word'"*[2].

She said, *"Yes."*

CHAPTER 2

Say Yes

M ost of us have difficulty relating to someone who achieves greatness. They become heroes, and their stories become legends that we can only hope to emulate. Society has elevated a wide range of people. Some admire athletes, or actors and actresses. Others closely follow great business leaders. Many look to politicians as the hope for better days ahead. The more significant the impact of the individual, the brighter their star shines, and the more distant they become from those of us observing their lives and achievements.

Abraham Lincoln, arguably one of our nation's greatest presidents, was a leader during one of the toughest times in United States history. The Civil War was threatening to split the nation in half, and President Lincoln is recognized and respected for his strong leadership. In the face of immense pressure, he reunited the states and abolished slavery. His place in history was solidified when he was assassinated following his victory. I don't know of one listing of great leaders that does not include his name. His achievements are incredible, and his star shines so brightly that it's hard to imagine ever living a life that compares.

Ordinary People

The reality is that before he was President Lincoln, he was just Abe, or Abraham to his mother. His life was so normal that it was indistinguishable from most of the lives around him. He was born to a poor family that suffered from sicknesses and financial difficulties. Through hard work, Abe eventually became a self-educated lawyer and possibilities began to open for him. But he still failed more than he succeeded. The only reason Abe Lincoln's life was any different than the names you will never know was his decision to say, *"Yes"* to opportunity.

Perspective is everything.

Today, Mary is honored as the mother of the Savior of mankind. In delivery rooms around the world, millions of parents greet the arrival of their newborn daughters, and then, with heavy emotion in their voice, say, *"Her name is Mary."* It might also surprise you that many parents gaze in wonder at their sons and name them after this girl Mary. They may say, *"We will name him Mario"* or *"His name will be Marion."*

They are honoring the mother of Jesus by naming their child after her. In some way, they may be hoping that this baby gains some of the strength and character of this young Jewish woman who was willing to say, *"yes"* to God's call. They may be praying that the little *"something"* that launched Mary into a unique and blessed life would attach itself to their offspring.

Perspective is everything. We may think from our current perspective that experiencing a life that has any similarity to Mary's would be impossible. That perception would be completely incorrect.

The incredible reality is that Mary was a completely ordinary Hebrew woman living an ordinary village life. Nazareth was not a major city or place of influence. It was on the southern outskirts of a much bigger city, Sepphoris. Those from Nazareth could walk about an hour to arrive in this bustling city. During Mary's lifetime, Sepphoris would have boasted a population of well over one thousand residents and been host to expansive building projects.

In contrast, Nazareth was a small agrarian town of between three and four hundred people. Archeology reveals it to be a village of well-spaced homes which allowed animals to be raised close to the families who owned them. The flocks and herds which grazed just outside the village would have probably been comprised of the combined assets of the residents. Historians tell us that Nazareth was made up of a few large families, so everyone probably knew everyone else. It was known to be a devout village that was not caught up in the trend toward Grecian thought and culture.

In Mary's world, a young woman didn't expect to advance in life except through a good marriage arrangement.

As a young woman, Mary was tasked with the usual chores of the day. She would wake up early and draw water from the well in the village center, prepare meals for the family, and feed the livestock. The rest of the day she spent cleaning the home, mending clothes, and learning how to be a good wife to the man she would one day marry.

Like many young people of our time who live in small towns, she may have entertained dreams of grand adventures. Maybe one day she would move to the city. As a devout Jew, she probably planned a visit to Jerusalem to worship in the woman's court of the temple.

A significant difference between the realities of Mary's time and ours is found in the possibility for advancement. Today it is not unusual to hear of a woman being raised in underprivileged surroundings only to find promotion through education and oc-cupation. Mary didn't have any such opportunities. As a woman, she would not have been allowed an education, so a promising career was out of the question. In Mary's world, a young woman didn't expect to advance in life except through a good marriage arrangement.

Mary was willing to entertain the idea that something great could be birthed from her life.

Before being visited by Gabriel, Mary was betrothed to Joseph, something that is uncommon these days. It was a step between our modern engagement and marriage. To disengage from a betrothal was generally the same as getting divorced. Doing so would result in a lifetime of dishonor and shame. Knowing the identity of her future husband gave Mary a good idea what her future would look like. Marrying Joseph meant becoming the wife of a skilled craftsman. While she would never be rich, she would also not be poor. Her life was going to be better than it would be if she had married a farmer, but it probably wasn't much of a step up the social ladder, and it certainly didn't speak to any greatness in her future.

The Difference Maker

Mary's life was utterly ordinary. Only one tiny thing separated her from any other young lady living in a small village in the hills of Galilee. She was willing to entertain the idea that something great could be birthed from her life.

Have you ever wondered how many young ladies lived along-side Mary in Galilee? I've often wondered if Mary was the first person that God sent Gabriel to talk to. God could have said, *"Gabriel ask Abigail if she is interested in bringing my son into*

the world. She is already in Bethlehem. It would be easy for her."
Maybe God said, *"Check with Martha over in Jerusalem. My plan is for My son to be born in Bethlehem and Jerusalem is just down the road. That could work out great!"* I wonder if God had Gabriel work his way north from Bethlehem visiting one virgin after another looking for a willing vessel. We can't know the answer to that, but we do know that he visited Mary. The only reason we know her name today is that she said *"yes"* to the opportunity.

What God is desiring to bring forth from your life will be unique to you.

Everyone agrees that Mary lived an incredible life and because of what she accomplished, some have attempted to elevate her to a godlike status. I think Mary would appreciate their respect but hate the implications. Scripture doesn't share much about Mary's life after Jesus took the spotlight, but it does give a special mention years later. After the crucifixion, burial, resurrection, and ascension of Jesus, we find 120 believers gathered in an upstairs room in Jerusalem. They were following the instructions of Jesus to wait for the promise of the Father. Scripture tells us within that group of fervent believers was Mary, the mother of Jesus.[3]

She had given birth to the Savior, supported Him through His life and ministry, suffered greatly as He died for the sins of humanity, and now prayed humbly for the promise from the Father. She, more than anyone, seemed to understand the value of any promise the Father made. No matter how impossible it sounded, Mary knew it would be worth waiting for.

A Calling Fulfilled

Mary was a great woman and a sinner who needed a Savior. What made her unique is that she was someone who completely fulfilled her calling from God. She was willing to do something so unique that it had never been done before, and it has not been done since. She is an inspiration and example for all of us.

Mary's calling was to have a baby. That may be impossible for you. It certainly is for me. What God birthed from the life of Mary was and is unique to her. What God is desiring to bring forth from your life will be unique to you. You can't and shouldn't try to duplicate the result of Mary's obedience to God. There is only one Savior, and He has already been born.

However, what Mary did spiritually, mentally, and emotionally is well within the realm of possibility for you. Mary's story is a template for anyone who is ready to give birth to the destiny God is calling them toward.

What is God asking you to deliver from your life? What destiny has God designed for you? Remember, God created you. He designed you from scratch. His calling for your life is just as unique as you are. Mary was uniquely qualified for her calling and so are you!

Designed for More

Unlike all other creatures on Earth, humanity is designed to change the surrounding environment. Scientists promote the amazing abilities of the many animals of the world. I've read articles about the creativity of the chimpanzee. There are several documentaries on the intelligence of the dolphin. Books have been written on the teamwork and organization of lion and wolf packs.

Even as we admire the animal kingdom, let's recognize that humanity is the only species studying the others. Humans are building, creating, discovering, and strategizing while the animal kingdom is hunting or gathering its next meal. Humanity is advancing knowledge and creatively changing its surroundings at a rapidly increasing speed.

Why does humanity operate at a higher level than other sentient beings? Because God designed us that way.

The original introductions of both God and mankind in scripture reveal some great truths.

The very first revelation of God shows Him as a creative being. Genesis 1:1 says, *"In the beginning God created the heavens and the earth"* [NLT]. Think about how incredible this statement is. *"In the beginning"* declares the start of a timeline. The word *"God"* reveals who this story is going to be about. The revelation of God is followed directly by the word *"created."* The impact of the order of these words should not be overlooked because they scream an essential truth about God: He is creative!

Something needs to be birthed from your life.

Our introduction to the idea of mankind occurs in Genesis 1:26. After developing the rest of creation by the command of His voice, God changes His pattern. *"God said, 'Let us make human beings in our image, to be like us.'"*[4] This was not said about any other part of creation. No great apes were spoken into existence. No intelligent dolphins were spoken into existence. It was only humanity that God said, *"Let's make them to look like us and be like us."* God then formed man from the dust of the Earth and breathed His own breath into Adam. Divinity was breathed into humanity as the Great Creator developed His crowning creation in His own image to be like Him.

I admire all of God's creation, but logic demands the recognition that humanity was not created equal with, but superior to, the rest of the sentient beings. We were created by a God who desired to be a Father to us. This meant humanity would share some of the same characteristics as its creator.

After creation, Adam was not left alone to follow his instincts. He was immediately given a job. God brought each of the animals before Adam. His job was to name them.

Naming a few children is no easy task. I can't imagine naming all of the animals. God could have named them, but He didn't.

God pulled at the creative nature of humanity from the moment Adam was created.

Immediately after Eve's creation, God did it again. He blessed Adam with Eve and immediately said, *"Be fruitful and multiply and fill the earth"*.[5] This was a command for the first couple to have children. From the beginning, God pulled personal creativity as well as collaborative creativity from humanity.

What Lies Within

God created you! His creativity is within you, and because you are reading this book, I believe He is calling it from you. You are designed to give birth! Children are part of God's plan for a family, but it's not the only birth that God has designed you for.

Within you lies new ideas, new companies, new strategies, new relationships, new Christians, new books, new blogs, new websites, new videos, new movies, new _____ *(you fill in the blank)*. What leapt to your mind as you read that list of what God could empower you to give birth to?

We move forward by birthing new things.

What I know for sure is that something needs to be birthed from your life. We move forward by birthing new things. If new children stopped coming into the world, humanity would cease to exist within 100 years. The same is true about invention, business development, church advancement, and almost anything else you can think of. Without birth, there is only death.

Mary was called to give birth to something incredible. I believe you are called to give birth to something incredible too! In the following chapters, we will look into Mary's experience in detail. By identifying and dissecting key events, we can apply them to our lives.

Let me take a moment to warn you, however. Mary's yes changed her life completely. No doubt, as Gabriel stood there waiting for an answer, Mary thought hard about what agreeing to God's plan could mean for her life. There was no way she could begin to imagine the story that would unfold before her. Nothing like this had ever happened before.

---

*God is calling you to give birth to something unique. Are you willing to say "**yes**"?*

Anything God is calling you to birth from your life will also be completely unique. It will not be unique in name, but it will be completely unique in essence. If God births a business from your life, it won't be the first business to ever exist. If God calls you to launch a church, it won't be the first church ever launched. God may call you to write a book, start a family, develop a movie, or write a song, and while none of these will be unique in name, it will remain unique in essence.

Most people have experienced the value of eating at McDonald's. Their value is built into their systems. Every store is almost identical. I can promise you that each one is built with identical processes, but they are also very unique. Their uniqueness lies in the identity of those owning and managing the franchise. I've experienced excellent service and remarkably clean facilities in one restaurant and had an entirely different experience just days later visiting another McDonald's.

What you birth from your life may be called by the same name as something that already exists, but don't think for a moment that it will be identical. The uniqueness is that they have not been built, developed, grown up, or been established by you in this time with this calling and in your present context. God is calling you to give birth to something unique. Are you willing to say *"yes"*?

Mary said, *"Yes,"* and that three-letter word launched her into an entirely new way of living.

PART 1

Conception

CHAPTER 3

Relationship Makes the Difference

I'm typing on a MacBook Pro. It is one of several in my house. Computers have become such a common part of life that it's hard to remember a time they didn't exist. The story of Apple is a particularly spectacular example of what ingenuity and hard work can achieve. Steve Jobs and Steve Wozniak *(or Woz as he's known)* worked together to create a company that is currently one of the greatest success stories in modern business. With the now iconic Apple symbol prominent in our minds, albums being released directly on iTunes, and the ubiquitous nature of all things *"i,"* it is hard to imagine this company as anything except the powerhouse of technology and innovation it has become. But Apple did not suddenly appear on the scene as a mega-corporation.

In the well-known story, the two Steves launched Apple in a house in Menlo Park, California. They didn't start a company then create their first computer. Instead, the company was established in response to Woz's creation of what would be known as the Apple 1.

Speaking to NPR *(National Public Radio)* in 2006, Woz explained that *"When I built this Apple I... the first computer to say a computer should look like a typewriter - it should have a keyboard - and the output device is a TV set, it wasn't really to show the world [that] here is the direction [it] should go [in]. It was to really show the people around me, to boast, to be clever, to get acknowledgement for having designed a very inexpensive computer."* [6]

Before there was an Apple Inc., there was an idea. This idea alone could not produce a great company. Wozniak was certainly inventive, but he didn't see the potential in what he had created. On his own, he would have shared his invention with his friends and family and reveled in their adoration. He would have enjoyed their exclamations of surprise as he explained and demonstrated how this invention worked. Maybe he would have personally developed the idea over the years, but it is likely that without Jobs, his invention would have gone no farther. It was when the idea was shared with the right person that Apple Inc. came into existence.

There are no shortcuts to your destiny.

Woz couldn't have created Apple on his own and Mary alone could not command the birth of Jesus. A child cannot be created by the will of one individual. Even today, with the miracle of modern medicine, two genetic codes are a requirement for new life.

Yes, God could have appeared on the Earth at any time. He had done so when appearing to Adam, Moses, and Abraham, but this time was different. Every time God showed up on Earth in human form, He was still entirely Divine. For God to achieve His desired outcome, His resulting manifestation had to be subject to natural realities. He had to get tired, hungry, feel pain, and ultimately die. Appearing to humanity would not accomplish those goals, so the eternal God became a literal man. So, *"when the right time came, God sent his Son, born of a woman, subject to the law."* [7] That Son's name was Jesus.

Start at the Beginning

The celebration of Christmas is focused on the birth of Jesus. This is both right and good, but His birth was not the beginning of the story. The birth was the result of a process that eventually led to the expression of Mary's destiny, but this is rarely discussed. It feels great to talk about holding your destiny in your hands. It's wonderful to think of seeing it take its first steps or saying its first words. It's exciting to think about your company earning its first dollar, your book making its first sale, or your song being sung for the first time. Keeping the end in mind is key to staying focused, but without the beginning, there can be no end. The end arrives through a process that always starts at the beginning.

There are no shortcuts to your destiny, and bypassing the process will leave you consistently disappointed. Eventually, you will give up altogether. Even God worked through the process.

Making salvation available to all mankind was big and bold. It was just a Divine idea until Mary agreed to God's plan and allowed the process to begin with the conception of a child in her womb.

The process of Apple's birth began when Jobs and Woz dreamt of what could be and made their first agreement to move forward together. That agreement was the conception of what would become Apple Inc.

Like Apple or Jesus, before your destiny can become a reality, conception must occur. Conception is the act of becoming pregnant. It is the initial step of everything that will ever be birthed from your life. Without conception, there is no expectation of birth.

When a woman says, *"I'm expecting!"* her husband doesn't assume a new car will be arriving soon. He understands that conception has occurred, and the wailing cries of a new life will soon echo through the home. A process has begun. Every new thing developed from human life begins with conception.

In the beginning, God created Adam from the dust of the Earth. God then blew into Adam the breath of life from His own being. I picture this event much like someone being given mouth to mouth resuscitation. God got personal with Adam and transferred what was within Himself into Adam. This transaction separated humanity from the rest of creation completely. God then put Adam to sleep and, taking a rib from his side, created Eve. Both Adam and Eve were creations of God using material He had already formed. The commands of God were few and simple. He said, *"Be fruitful and multiply. Fill the earth and govern it."*[8]

Fruitfulness was a commandment from God. Being creative, He expected humanity, created in His image, to be creative as well. Had God not commanded fruitfulness from mankind, they would have been fruitful anyway. Whether it was the sexual desires that conceived children or the human interaction resulting in natural collaboration, humanity was created to be fruitful. God had created man in His own image to be like Him. His own creative nature was going to manifest itself in mankind. An innate desire for creative interaction was placed within humanity and conception would be the result.

In Adam and Eve's case, we read, *"Now Adam had sexual relations with his wife, Eve, and she became pregnant."*[9] Just like today, conception resulted from relationship. Once conception has taken place, expectation can begin because a process has started.

False Pregnancy

One of the saddest conditions is a false pregnancy. This condition doesn't often occur in humans, but it is relatively common in the animal kingdom.

Years ago, my wife Kristy and I had a small Cairn Terrier named Poe. She was not the brightest dog in the world, but she was very sweet, fluffy, and about the size of a small stuffed animal. She was so tiny that she could only sleep in the bed with us if we remembered to lift her up. Poe was not particularly attached to toys, so when she developed a major attachment to a tiny stuffed Winnie the Pooh, we took notice.

Overnight this little bear became her whole world. At first, we noticed that she was disappearing into our closet and rummaging around. When we checked it out, we were surprised to find various articles from around the house had been assembled into a vague circle. Poe was laying in that circle with her Winnie the Pooh bear. She would stay there for hours at a time. She would come out to eat and then quickly return to the circle. If we touched her bear, she would whine and jump up as high as possible trying to get to the stuffed animal.

One day, we reached into the closet, and she growled. That's when we took her to the veterinarian to find out what was wrong with her. The vet heard our story and explained that Poe was experiencing a false pregnancy. She was spayed and could not have puppies, but for some reason, her body was convinced that something was within her and ready to be born. When the birth didn't happen, she fixated on the Winnie the Poo.

We did everything we could to make her comfortable after the doctor assured us that this would pass in time. Kristy and I pampered her for a few months while she lived out this fantasy, and then she returned to her usual self. Though it's sad enough watching an animal go through this, it is much sadder to watch men and women live out a false pregnancy of ideas for years.

Some false pregnancies occur with the promises of others.

Like Poe, they are believers. They believe that something great is going to happen in their lives, that they have a specific future before them. They speak in definite terms about what will occur in just a few short months or years. They are convinced that something beautiful is developing within them and prepare for birth. I've witnessed people devote themselves and their resources to the preparation of something that will never arrive, never realizing that conception must occur before expectation can be valid.

Some of these false pregnancies occur with the promises of others. Twice I've been given promises by those I trusted only to be greatly disappointed when what I thought was being born didn't materialize. I heard and believed their words without recognizing that conception had never taken place. The emotional and financial cost took years to recover from.

False pregnancy can also occur when someone is trying to escape the negative reality of their situation by sheer mental willpower. When their circumstance becomes unbearable, they convince themselves that something great is just around the corner. Without conception, this type of wishful thinking only results in greater levels of disappointment than ever before.

False pregnancy will only convince you of an impossible expectation. Expectation alone is unrewarding. Eternally expecting, but never giving birth, is a horrible way to live. Yet, many Christians live lives of one false pregnancy after another.

Identifying False Pregnancies

You can identify false pregnancies in your life by listening to the words you speak. Luke tells us, *"...What you say flows from what is in your heart."*[10] If you regularly refer to what is *"about to happen"* and not what *"is happening,"* you may be experiencing a false pregnancy.

In certain circles of Christianity, it is common to hear phrases like, *"God's about to (fill in the blank with the expected thing) in my life!"* They may declare that God is about to bless them in a big way this week only to declare Divine intervention the next. When pressed, they will often find a way to explain away the fact that what they were expecting did not occur like they declared it would.

If this describes your reality, then you are living in persistent expectation without the possibility of achieving your expected outcome. Conception must occur in your life!

Christians reading this book may question my belief in the miraculous power of God. You may remind me that the Christian life is dominated by faith. You may remind me that, as Christians, we live a life based upon faith. I would agree with you completely. At its core, faith is an actionable belief in something unseen.

Christianity does not exist without faith. Christianity would also not exist if Mary had declared she would have a baby but left out the conception part. Belief without undergoing this process does not result in birth, with the single exception of a miraculous event.

Christianity does not exist without faith.

Yes, in the scripture Paul tells us, *"..we live by believing and not by seeing."*[11] This means that there will always be an expectation of something we cannot yet see. Some use this verse to explain away the possibility of a false pregnancy. Paul is describing the assurance of an eternal home in Heaven even though we can't see it yet. He is not writing about spending your life consistently hoping for things that never occur.

Our expectation is the foundation of our outlook on the future. A false expectation of something beautiful results in disappointment while false expectation of something terrible results in preparation and consistent dread. Expectation depends on a resolution, and that resolution is the eventual birth of something.

Your offspring is your tie to the future. My sons connect me to a future I will never see, but I am affecting. The birth of a healthy company positively impacts the future of the founder and their family. The birth of a good book leaves something that could last for generations. The birth of a successful church offers the knowledge that you played a part in expanding God's kingdom and affecting eternity.

Many thousands of years before the birth of Apple Inc. or even Jesus, there was the birth of a nation. We now honor the Jewish nation of Israel, but like every nation, it had a starting point. Israel began with one man and one woman. I'm not entirely sure why God chose Abraham to become the father of this great nation, and I like not knowing. If I knew why God chose Abraham, I might try to duplicate Abraham's life. Trying to become like Abraham could disqualify my life for the calling God has for me. The same is true for you.

The first chapter of Matthew lists off the genealogy from Abraham to Jesus. This is followed by the opening words of Jesus's story. Matthew reveals that Joseph was struggling with believing the source of Mary's pregnancy. As her fiancé, who was doing everything properly, his struggle is understandable. I'd love to say I would have believed Mary, but it's not every day that your fiancé announces that she's soon to give birth to the Savior of the world. I'm not sure I'd have believed her. God visited Joseph in a dream. This dream was significant because it not only brought peace to Joseph, but it also clarified the process Mary went through to give birth to the Savior.

An angel said to Joseph in a dream, *"Joseph, son of David... do not be afraid to take Mary as your wife. For the child within her was conceived by the Holy Spirit."*[12] The angel confirmed that Mary's expectation was valid and that conception had taken place.

The expectation is exciting, but pointless without conception. If you are expecting, I pray there has been a conception.

The process of conception is so important that we will spend the next few chapters breaking down the three elements necessary for it to take place. We will look at them in some detail along with a few things that prevent conception in our lives. I pray that applying Mary's experience to your life will empower you to move into the destiny God has designed for you.

It's time to conceive your future!

CHAPTER 4

Intimacy Isn't Easy

I am something of a prude. In this era, speaking openly about the most intimate parts of life is common. I'm still not comfortable with talking about some things, and years ago, I was much worse.

In our second year of marriage, Kristy and I decided to expand our family by having a child. I'd given Kristy a cat the previous year we had named Jeeves. He was a great kitten and our first attempt as a couple at keeping something helpless alive. Seeing that Jeeves was still going strong, we figured our chances of success with a child were fairly high - as long as we weren't trying to potty-train him or her with the litter box. At some point, Kristy looked at me with a big smile and said, *"I'm pregnant!"*

In that moment, I wish I could tell you that I was excited to become a father. I wish I could say I was overcome with fierce protection for the love of my life as she carried our child. I would like to report that I thanked God for answering our prayers. I'd like to tell you anything except the truth. My first thought upon hearing that Kristy was pregnant was, *"Oh no! Now people are going to know for sure that we are having sex!"*

We had been married for two years. Our love life was not something anyone was either concerned about or questioning. In my mind, however, we were removing any doubt.

Why was I so sure our not-so-secret secret was out? The moment we made our announcement, or when Kristy began to show signs of her expectation, certain assumptions would be made. If they are expecting, then there must have been a conception, and that cannot occur without intimacy.

The Intimacy Requirement

This is what made Mary's situation so difficult. She was a virgin. She had not been intimate with anyone. She was going to have a lot of explaining to do.

The questions were many. Was Joseph going to understand how this pregnancy occurred? How would her family receive the news? How would society respond to something that they could not understand?

They would assume she had been intimate with a man. She would be denying the claim while showing every known evidence to the contrary. This sure wasn't going to be easy!

Yes, the birth of Jesus was miraculous, but it still required intimacy. While Mary did not have an intimate moment with a man, she experienced intimacy with the Holy Spirit. From the beginning, God determined that for conception to occur, intimacy would be required, and the conception of Jesus was no different.

Scripture tells of how the Holy Spirit covered Mary.[13] In Greek, this word gives the understanding of something wrapping itself around another. In other words, the Holy Spirit wrapped Himself around Mary. I don't want to paint a sexual picture here, but for life to have been created, there must have been intimacy.

In this moment with the Spirit of God, something was planted within Mary's womb and joined with the product of her own body. This incredible moment resulted in something becoming alive within her. Nine months later, Mary would hold a child in her arms and call Him Jesus, and it all began with intimacy. The conception of your destiny will begin the same way!

The vision of your life may be birthing a company, a book, a relationship, or a church. Intimacy is still required. Without it, new life can never be conceived.

In this hyper-sexualized culture, we must remove the sexual component from the term intimacy. Intimacy simply indicates closeness. It reveals a moment when one allows themselves to be close enough to another person to allow the natural barriers to lower. As this happens, the more real each becomes with the other until there is a true understanding of themselves revealed.

In our world, intimacy usually means being physically naked, but emotional and intellectual openness are far more important than physical nakedness.

Intimacy simply indicates closeness.

It is easy to understand the intimacy necessary for the conception of a child, but this moment occurs in every type of conception.

Intimacy occurs when you share the secret hope of your heart. Maybe it's with a trusted friend or a loved one. A moment comes when you finally say out loud your hopes for the future. Maybe it's moment in conversation with a business partner that you first speak your vision for the new life that could be.

There will come a point in time to plant a seed into an environment where it will be nurtured, protected, and begin to grow. Without this environment, the seed will remain ineffective. Without being planted, the seed's greatness will never be realized. Planting always occurs in an intimate moment.

This moment creates the opportunity for complimenting things to collide and create new life. It may be a new career, a new club, a new business, or yes -- a new family. Intimacy brings the opportunity for the collision to take place.

In my life, these moments have primarily occurred in times of openness in communication with God followed by conversations with my wife.

In early 2001, Kristy and I began examining our church environment. I had been taught to value the church and its leadership highly, so I never critiqued either of them. These conversations were just that... conversations. We were young, idealistic, hardworking, and diligent believers who were suddenly looking at their church environment critically for the first time, and we held nothing back.

A key component of this story was that we were also spending time in prayer. We were not doing well financially, and it kept us both humble and prayerful, but God was providing for us daily in miraculous ways. In hindsight, it was both a stressful and a beautiful time. One thing was clear, however; our life was changing.

As months passed, we discovered something unique was occurring within our conversations. Our vocabulary began to shift. We moved from language describing our present reality to language describing what our reality could become. We began to address the issues we observed and spoke of a church environment where these issues would never arise at all.

Understand, we were not looking to become senior pastors anytime soon, and it wasn't in our minds to become church planters. The reality was that this time of consistent intimate prayer, combined with the ideological intimacy between Kristy and I, was resulting in a new idea being planted.

An intimate encounter is necessary to discover the potential of anything fresh and new locked away inside your life. There must be a moment when you drop your guard. A moment when you willingly share your deepest thoughts, dreams, visions, and ambitions. The anticipation of this moment is often accompanied by fear and anxiety.

You know the time is coming. It's a moment where you combine what you hope and envision with what you feel. This intimate moment is often so powerful that it can even result in new personal revelation.

I'll never forget an intimate moment of mine that occurred in 1988. It happened many miles and many years from where I am today. I was twelve, and we were living in the little town of

Kinston, North Carolina. In those days, the church participated in regular prayer meetings. This time it was on Friday night. I was kneeling on the floor with my hands and face resting on a pew covered in thick red fabric. My sister Regan was sitting on the pew next to where I was praying. I was telling Jesus how much I loved Him and wanted to serve Him. It was then that my monologue became a dialog. For the first time in my life, I knew that Jesus was speaking back to me.

The key to intimacy is a willingness to be open.

I didn't hear a voice in my head like James Earl Jones or Morgan Freeman. It was clear and pierced through my thoughts and the sounds in the room. *"You will preach my word."* It was short, simple, and life-changing. It was in this moment of intimate expression of my love and adoration for Him that Jesus chose to speak to me. It was the moment I knew for the first time that I was called to be a minister of the gospel of Jesus Christ.

As this revelation swept over my heart and mind, I looked up at my sister. Regan is only 18 months younger than me, so we have always been close. Overwhelmed by what was happening, I cried, *"Regan, God just called me into the ministry!"* Her response was equally simple and clear, *"So what?"* She then went back to her own prayers.

Not exactly the reception I was hoping for, but that moment of intimacy birthed something within me that has shaped my life to this very day.

When Things Go Wrong

Though conceptions have occurred when willing openness was not present, the process was violent, tedious, painful, and ultimately damaged the one conceiving. We call this process rape, and there is no intimacy involved.

There are those who have not been physically abused, but the violation of their life is just as real. I am not equating the emotional trauma and pain of a person who has been physically assaulted with that of someone who has had an idea forced upon them. I am saying that there are different types of drama and pain, and if someone is forced to conceive something unwillingly, there are negative repercussions.

I think about Ben and Samantha, a young, hard-working couple living in an apartment with their 8-month-old son. Their income could not cover their expenses. Just when it seemed like bankruptcy was on the horizon, they received word that their landlord was raising the rent on their apartment. While looking for alternative living arrangements, they met a leasing agent who was also a realtor. He suggested that they buy a house instead of renting. Ben and Samantha didn't think buying was possible, but after seeing nothing they could afford to rent, they agreed to check it out.

To their surprise, the realtor called the next day and offered to show them a house. Out of desperation, they began the process of making this house fit their life. They didn't like the house, couldn't afford the house, didn't care for the neighborhood or the neighbors, but they felt it was their only option. Soon after moving in, they realized that the house needed major repairs. In the first week, Ben found dime bags of white powder hidden above the door jams of the kitchen. That summer they discovered that the air condition unit was too small. In the hot California summer, their house was a furnace, and their electric bill was too high to afford.

Ben and Samantha were forced into a process that consistently brought more levels of pain and sorrow. The idea was forced upon them, and the process brought little benefit. Owning their first house should have been a momentous occasion. They should have celebrated the fact that it could happen at all. Instead, the process included nothing but stress, anxiety, and frustration.

This is an example of conceiving and giving birth to something without the benefit of intimacy.

Intimacy will not remove all the pain of giving birth, but it should be a beautiful precursor to the process. It's a moment of exhaling something into the universe that could change the world.

Unfortunately, many people never live out this beautiful moment. Maybe you are one who fears being that open and vulnerable, so you close yourself off to the possibility. Without openness, your life will remain the same.

My uncle Barry Sutton is a great leader and pastor. He has spoken to many thousands of people around the world, preaching the gospel with boldness. However, he wasn't always willing to be so open.

When he and my father Bobby were young, Barry needed a job. My father drove him to the local McDonalds to fill out an employment application. As he approached the counter, he became anxious about asking the counter staff for an application. A few moments later he jumped back into the car and quietly ate a hamburger.

My father asked him how it had gone. Barry's reply was non-committal. Bobby said, *"Did you fill out an application?"* Barry said no. Bobby asked, *"What did you do then?"* He said, *"I walked to the counter and ordered a hamburger."*

How many people are eating hamburgers when they would rather be earning money? How many are working for others when God has granted them the dream of self-employment. How many are making do with life simply because they are unwilling to allow an intimate moment to occur?

You may be thinking that asking for an application is not an intimate moment. I believe it is. The one asking for the application is revealing much about themselves. They are revealing they are lacking something. They are revealing their need. Their choice of location reveals where they believe they are along the ladder of opportunity. They are revealing much and are at the mercy of the one they are speaking to. That level of revelation causes the search for a job and the interview process to be one of the greatest creators of stress and anxiety for many people. However, without creating the opportunity for intimacy, they will remain unemployed.

Intimacy is not easy which is why so many have bottled up dreams and caged ambitions.

Fear of that intimate moment stops many from achieving all that God has placed within them. Fear caused by past events can stop you from dreaming. Fear of abandonment can cause you to create barriers to any sense of intimacy. Hurts of yesterday can cause you to refuse the possibilities of tomorrow.

Intimacy is not easy which is why so many have bottled up dreams and caged ambitions. The step into the intimate moment is so difficult that it produced Mary's only question.

In the entire story of Mary's visit from the angel Gabriel, she asked only one question: *"But how can this happen? I am a virgin."* Let's remember, for a moment, that the angel had just told Mary that she would give birth to the Savior of humanity who would reign over His kingdom forever. There are a few questions I can think to ask, but apparently, Mary was only worried about the intimacy required in conception.

Mary was saying, *"I've not experienced the intimacy necessary to give birth to anything. What you are describing requires an intimacy that I don't understand."*

I know that intimacy is scary. Hurts happen to everyone. You can stay right where you are, and few will question your choice. I, however, have one question for you. Do you want to be identified by your hurts or by your baby?

CHAPTER 5

Unity Is Necessary

Intimacy is the first step toward conception, but it is not the only challenge you will face.

We know the Holy Spirit overshadowed Mary. In this intimate moment, something was planted within Mary's womb which joined with the product of her own body. The result was the beginning of a new life.

I pray you will experience this type of intimacy in your life, that you will let down your guard and share your greatest imaginations with someone you trust. For that moment to result in conception, however, there must be unity in the intimacy.

A second party will always be involved in the conception process. The unity of a man and woman conceives physical children. The unity of a man and God conceives a different type of birth. The unity of an individual and the church conceives the family of God. The unity of Jobs and Woz conceived Apple. The spiritual and conceptual unity between Kristy and I conceived Legacy Church.[14]

In 2005, our family moved to the Big Island of Hawaii. We intended to plant a church in the city of Hilo, but God had other plans. After being on the island for about three weeks, a small church of 17 asked if we would consider being their pastors. While we were honored by the request, the group was in Kona-- on the other side of the island. Becoming their pastor meant changing our plans. After spending some time in prayer, we both felt the opportunity was right. We met with the group, and our plans changed.

Soon after agreeing to become the pastor, we learned that everything was not as it seemed. The previous pastor was a good man, but the church had not developed as he had hoped. This small group was in a lot of debt and not in a great relationship with the landlord of the building they leased. After speaking to an attorney, it was decided that we would close the church, pay its debts, and plant a new church. These three statements describe months of agonizing, strategizing, and a whole lotta of prayer.

We did not know how the group would respond. They could simply walk away, but we hoped and prayed they would stay with us for the launch of a new organization. The one certainty was the unity between Kristy and I. During those uncertain days, we used to say, *"It might be you and me under a coconut tree, but we will be together."*

We were blown away when this incredible group, now thirty-five strong, responded beautifully. Legacy Church was born. That group of people unified to launch a church that saw miraculous growth and development. We experienced incredibly difficult times together. We first survived and then we thrived. Today, Legacy Church has hundreds of believers who meet each week. It has a beautiful location, great music, biblical teaching, and strong leadership. Hawaii is not an easy place to launch a church, especially for a non-local, but God's grace was and is sufficient. It is a success story that initially hinged on the unity between Kristy and I, but that unity was not always our story.

When There is No Unity

Only four years before the launch of Legacy Church, our story was completely different. In 2001, we had moved from California to the town of Lombard, Illinois, a small western suburb of Chicago. I was twenty-five years old. Kristy was twenty-two and eight months pregnant with our second son. In conversation, we seemed to be on the same page. We sold our home, loaded our belongings into a moving truck, and made the journey halfway across the country. During the move, we seemed to have no issues with each other, but once we'd arrived in Lombard, things began to change.

Our new home was in the basement of a converted house turned church. The upstairs was the sanctuary, and the basement held the classrooms for children, as well as a bathroom. We planned to live in one of the basement rooms while building the congregation. Only days after we unloaded our truck into the basement, I leapt into the work of building a church. I didn't waste even a week getting my family settled or making sure my eight-month-pregnant wife was comfortable. I thought, *"The faster we build a congregation, the faster we can live comfortably."* I loved my wife, but I was proving to be a poor husband.

As the weeks, months, and years went by, Kristy became increasingly frustrated with me. We were holding two Sunday services and a Wednesday service. I was also teaching seventeen personal Bible studies per week in individual homes. I was working like crazy, but after two years, we only had a congregation of about twenty-five people. To top it off, our marriage was falling apart.

I could not understand what the issue was. In my mind, we were building a church for Jesus. I was playing my part by reaching new people, teaching studies, and preaching three times a week. Kristy was maintaining our one-room apartment, taking care of our children, and teaching the few children who would attend on Sundays. All the pieces for what should have been a successful launch of a church seemed to be in place, but things weren't getting better, only worse.

After two and a half years in the basement of the church, both Kristy and I went into the secular job market. We were blessed to both finds jobs quickly, and we soon bought a nice home. I thought everything was going to be better, but I was wrong. The church grew slowly, but Kristy and I were quickly becoming more and more distant.

One day, while walking home from work, I began thinking about what life would look like without Kristy in it. I was still pondering this possibility as I walked into the house. Kristy was already home, and I found her looking at apartments in the newspaper. She was also pondering life after divorce. The crazy reality was that we desperately loved each other. We loved our boys. We loved our family. We were in love, but we were falling apart.

This is the point I want to make clear: Kristy and I never stopped loving each other. We remained friends and lovers, but we were not unified.

It is the unity of the vision in your heart, skills you have gained, passion you possess, and the DNA you carry that makes what you are birthing unique.

Intimacy implies unity, but that is not always the reality. We were physically intimate, but we were not unified in our efforts to build a life and were considering ending the marriage completely. This would have likely put an end to the many great things God has since done with us and through us. There may have still been a church built in Kona, but it would not have been Legacy. It is the unity of the vision in your heart, skills you have gained, passion you possess, and the DNA you carry that makes what you are birthing unique. God's Spirit combined with Mary's DNA to create a wholly unique individual, Jesus. Without Mary's willingness to unify with God's vision and desire, she would have never given birth to Jesus.

There are hindrances to unity even when intimacy is present.

A number of years ago, Kristy and I were privileged to counsel a couple who were having difficulty conceiving a child. They had participated in fertility tests and treatments, but nothing seemed to be working. Eventually, the wife confessed to her husband that through it all she had been taking birth control pills. Due to doctor-patient confidentiality laws, he had never been told. The time, expense, and emotional toll were all for nothing because she was secretly blocking conception. They were intimate, but they were not unified in their desire for children. She didn't want him to be upset with her, so she went through the motions without intending ever to conceive.

I believe that those reading this book desire something greater: to make a difference with your life, to establish something greater than yourself which will outlive you.

The process for conception is simple and even hardwired into the DNA of humanity. It's why our population continues to grow. The desire to create is part of the human condition, but choosing the right partner is more difficult.

Becoming intimate is an exhilarating experience. It's fun! Modern medical technology has made it possible to experience the fun and exhilaration of intimacy without having to fear the responsibility of conception. This created a culture that feels at liberty to participate in moments of intimacy without considering unity. One-night stands aren't planning to bring a new life, a new idea, a fresh concept, a strong business, or family into the world.

I believe that those reading this book desire something greater: to make a difference with your life, to establish something greater than yourself which will outlive you. A one-night stand mentality will not accomplish that goal. You are looking for intimacy with unity. Nothing less will do. Finding that partner is not easy, but it is worth the effort.

Unity is not always achieved immediately. Sometimes achieving unity is an all-out war. It's also worth the battle.

After Kristy and I both realized we were thinking seriously about divorce, our arguments changed. Until this point, they had been blazing hot. There was lots of yelling and plenty of tears, but in hindsight, we had been circling the same arguments. Now all pretensions were gone. We started communicating on an entirely new level. I was sharing things I'd never said to her before, and so was she.

While these things hurt deeply, this was us communicating at our most honest. At some point, we realized that, while we loved each other, we were not unified. Then the conversation shifted from ending the marriage to what life could be like if we were working together.

Come Together

Over the years, we have been complimented often on our teamwork. Rarely am I involved in something that Kristy is not fully engaged with. She may not attend the meetings or speak with the teams, but her influence is very real. The same can be said of me concerning her efforts. When we receive these compliments, I often flash back to the days when it all looked like it was over. I smile inside and thank God for His goodness. We have a great marriage. We are a team. These things are true because intimacy is now combined with unity.

---

*Saying, **"Yes"** to destiny means risking all that you know and possess.*

When we left the Chicago area to plant a church in Hawaii, we were still the same people, but we were now unified in purpose. Maybe it's no surprise that about nine months later Legacy Church was born.

Unity is not an easy thing to develop. You may be a blessed person with many people in your life who are willing to dream along with you. Finding the person who is willing to move past their present point with you is more difficult. Saying, *"Yes"* to destiny means risking all that you know and possess. Developing that unified partnership willing to take that step with you is challenging.

Developing a Unified Partnership

I can't tell you exactly what to look for because what fits one personality may not fit another. The person who matches me may drive you completely out of your mind, but I can help you identify some key traits.

I call the first one the *"can't"* syndrome. These people feel it's their job to *"keep your feet on the ground."* These are some of the most difficult people to handle because they are often close to you. They hear the vision and usually sound supportive at first. They may say, *"Wow! That's a grand vision! It would be great if that were to happen."* Just as you think they are going to unify with making that happen, they say, *"..., but that can't happen because..."*

Sometimes they say, *"...that can't..."* while at other times they say, *"...you can't..."* The difficulty is that you know they mean well. They care about you.

I have been very close to my grandfather, Alfred Stephens, my entire life. He graduated from this Earth on April 5, 2015. No one on Earth believed in me more than my Pawpaw *(grandpa for non-southerners)*. When we knew we were leaving Chicago to plant a church in Hawaii, I was excited to bring him in on the plan. He heard me out and said, *"Well, if that's what you think you need to do. I just hope you don't go over there to starve and die. You have a family to think about."*

I couldn't believe it! I was confused. He was one of my greatest champions, and while he didn't try to stop me, he certainly expressed his doubts. He would have been happy if I had stayed away from Hawaii altogether. I could not allow his *"can't"* to impact me. There was a dream at stake. There was a destiny to be birthed. I knew then that he was not one I could unify with on this dream.

Flashing forward a few years and it was one of my great privileges to see him sitting in a service at Legacy Church with tears streaming down his face. I can still hear his voice saying, *"I'm proud of you, Micah."*

Pawpaw loved me completely, but the *"can't"* consumed him concerning that vision. You aren't looking for someone who is blind to the issues and limitations. You are looking to unify with someone who sees the obstacle and begins searching for the way to overcome it. You are looking to unify with someone who can capitalize on a hidden opportunity within the obstacle.

Before unity can be attained with another, it must be achieved between yourself and the God that has developed that vision within you. You may not be battling with the *"can't"* syndrome from the outside. You may be the one saying, *"I can't."* At some point, you must be able to see your own ability to conceive the dream and birth the vision. Otherwise, you have lost before you've begun. I believe many people abandon their destiny before it ever has an opportunity to be conceived.

Before unity can be attained with another, it must be achieved between yourself and the God that has developed that vision within you.

The idea begins to form, and like Mary's experience, the Holy Spirit begins to wrap Himself around their minds and hearts, giving them the capacity to experience something miraculous. In this moment, the possibility becomes overwhelming. Before they ever speak a word to anyone around them to build unity outside of themselves, they remove themselves from the process.

The words, *"I just can't"* are left ringing into an abyss of what might have been.

The old saying goes, *"If you think you can or think you can't, you're right."* You must be able to see yourself conceiving and birthing your destiny for it to come to pass. If you aren't there yet, I encourage you to close this book. Knowledge of the birthing process may encourage you to try to skip by the development of unity within intimacy.

The reality is that, long before Kristy and I arrived in Chicago, we were not unified in our vision for life. By planting without unity, we almost destroyed our marriage and the dream. It was only after gaining unity within our intimacy that we were able to move forward successfully.

Mutual Submission

The New Testament teaches the unique concept of mutual submission. In most human interactions, there is the boss with all the authority and everyone under them. In God's society, however, He directs us to submit ourselves one to another.[15] The writer Paul declares God's will within the church structure and then specifically in marriage. Mutual submission is not a lack of structural hierarchy of any kind. Paul clearly teaches a hierarchy of the home in the following verses, and other areas of the New Testament include instructions for the hierarchy of the church. What is unique about God's hierarchy is that the one in authority is commanded to be the servant of the one they lead.

If we look at the life of Jesus, we see this clearly. Jesus is the head of the church. He created it, declared that it was His church, and leads it today.[16] He has all authority over the church, but He also gave His life for it. He was the leader of the church and its greatest servant.

Concerning the hierarchy of the household, Paul writes that wives should submit to their husbands. This would seem to say that the husband is the *"boss."* He also says that the husband is to love the wife like Christ loves the church in that, *"He gave His life for her."*[17] So, the wife should submit to the husband, and the husband should be willing to die for the wife. Who is really in charge if the *"boss"* gives up their very life for those serving under them? This is mutual submission in action!

This mutual submission is key to any unity. When I realized what I was doing to Kristy, we addressed my schedule. We established a *"family day"* that we have kept since then. We developed a lasting plan of communication. There have been many occasions when Kristy has chosen to submit her opinion to me. There have been just as many when I have submitted my opinion to her. This is how unity is developed and maintained.

Without submission, unity will never exist. Without unity, intimacy will never result in conception. Without conception, expectation will never be valid. Without expectation, a delivery will never occur.

Mary had a choice to make. Would she choose her own path for life, or allow God's calling to become her reality? Mary chose to say, *"I am the Lord's servant. May everything you have said about me come true."*[18] Had she chosen any other course, her name would likely have been forgotten. She is remembered because she chose unity with God's will for her life. She chose servanthood.

You can choose to be the *"boss"* of a meager future if you desire. I believe your destiny is bigger than that! A *"we"* attitude will birth more than an *"I"* attitude ever could.

CHAPTER 6

Timing is Everything

The great American comedian Eddie Cantor coined a line that has been used by many successful people. He said, *"It takes twenty years to create an overnight success."*

I first heard something similar from Taylor Swift in a documentary about her life and career. Years ago, she was stopped by a reporter after winning several awards. The reporter asked what it was like becoming an overnight success. Taylor replied, *"I have worked very hard for a long time to become an overnight success."*

Miss Swift's answer stuck with me. With wisdom beyond her years, she expressed an acute understanding of the moment she was living in. She had worked hard writing songs, playing music, and pursuing agents. While she was still a young lady, her efforts had begun as a young girl. When her friends were playing, she was writing. When others her age were having fun, she was pursuing agents. All that work was now paying dividends. She had gone through a process and knew that timing was a big factor in her budding stardom.

Taylor was not the first to experience a process blessed with fortunate timing. Mary's experience was similar. The scripture tells us, *"...when the right time came, God sent his Son, born of a woman, subject to the law."* [19] This process was time sensitive.

Mary was available at the right time, and that fact was going to bless her life and change the course of humanity.

Timing is critical in the birth of your destiny. Conception occurs in cycles. Some people become frustrated and walk away from their destiny because they don't see anything happening. They are trying to be open to God's calling. They are wholly unified with God's plan for their life. Everything seems to be right, but they know nothing is alive within them. The timing must be correct for your destiny to be conceived.

A Matter of Timing

I hate the *"timing talk."* That's what I call it when someone takes me aside to tell me that what I was longing for would happen, but this wasn't the right time. It seemed to me that the right time never arrived! This *"timing talk"* seemed like a great way to calm down a young man who was eager to see his dreams and visions come to pass. It was a cliché response to gut-wrenching frustration. It was something I could see coming from a mile away, and I hated it. The fact that I despised the *"timing talk"* didn't make it wrong. It made me normal – maybe you are too. Now seeing some of my dreams in hindsight, I recognize the importance of timing. I still don't like to wait, but it frustrates me less than it used to.

When a woman decides she wants to become pregnant, she records her menstrual cycle. She knows that outcomes of sexual intimacy vary depending on where she is in her fertility cycle. In the natural world, the window of opportunity to conceive is only forty-eight hours each month. This is the timespan of viability for the egg that has been released into the womb. If a healthy connection is made during those forty-eight hours, then conception occurs. If a connection does not happen, then roughly twenty-eight days will pass before conception is possible again.

Each month, the woman's body will prepare itself for conception. If those forty-eight hours pass without it, her body will prepare for the process all over again. If conception fails to occur in the first few months, most couples don't mind. It's when the months and sometimes years go by without success that frustration can set in. In some cases, this can lead to emotional challenges as they continue to pursue the dream of conceiving a child.

The same challenge can affect dreamers like you and me. You know God has placed something unique deep within you. You're doing everything you can to allow for conception but haven't experienced that first sign of things moving forward. I hate to tell you this, but I must. Conception doesn't occur on command. It happens only when the timing of all the parts align.

Consider the timing of Jesus's birth. Some have tied this *"right time"* to the historical realities of Mary's day. The Roman Empire was spreading across the known world. The building of roads and the introduction of a common language was linking previously isolated areas and allowing the gospel to spread farther faster. I don't pretend to know all that God meant by defining this moment as the *"right time."* I do know that by defining a *"right time,"* scripture reveals that a *"wrong time"* existed as well.

> *Conception doesn't occur on command. It happens only when the timing of all the parts align.*

The timing of Jesus had to be very specific to align with the prophecies of His birth. Let's just take one prophetic statement and think through the timing issues involved. The prophet Micah *(who, you might imagine, is one of my favorites)* said, *"But you, O Bethlehem Ephrathah, are only a small village among all the people of Judah. Yet a ruler of Israel, whose origins are in the distant past, will come from you on my behalf."*[20] The prophecy said the Savior would be born in Bethlehem.

This doesn't sound very impressive until we remember that Mary lived in Nazareth. In these days, few people traveled more than a few miles from home. Those that did venture into the unknown rarely returned to their birthplace because travel was such an arduous process. Purposefully traveling with a pregnant woman was certainly unusual. It seemed like God's plan contained a fatal flaw. The virgin He chose was a very long way from the place He chose.[21] It seemed like the timing here was very wrong.

God's ways and thoughts are beyond our understanding. We can't imagine the reality He works within. We can see the results of His thoughts and ways as they are enacted on Earth. At some point, long before Gabriel visited Mary, a conversation began in Rome. This conversation likely went through many stages until the Emperor of Rome made a major decision and proclamation. Caesar declared that every man in the empire would be required to return to the town in which he was born to pay taxes.

God's ability to orchestrate time did not stop after the birth of Jesus. If the dream within you is one He is blessing, He is working out the timing in your life too!

This was unheard of. It hugely disrupted citizens all across the Empire. People who usually remained close to home were now traveling to places they had not visited for many, many years. Traders who lived in what is now known as the United Kingdom were traveling through the Mediterranean Sea to ports in northern Africa. Some living in modern France would be traveling to modern Turkey. This decree moved people from across the known world. Overland travel speeds of that time would have consisted of between eight and twenty miles per day depending upon weather, roadway conditions, and the health of the traveler.

Even if Joseph and Mary had chosen the fastest route and traveled at the fastest speeds, the journey would have taken at least four days. Add to that the fact that Mary was pregnant and probably riding a donkey while Joseph walked, the trip probably took longer than that.

Consider how incredible it was for Rome to launch the rollout of a major, world-changing tax directive within the timeframe of Mary's nine-month-long conception and delivery. The chance that the timing of all these moving pieces would randomly coincide is incredibly small. Yes, this is a miracle of God's timing. God's ability to orchestrate time did not stop after the birth of Jesus. If the dream within you is one He is blessing, He is working out the timing in your life too!

Giving and Receiving

The challenge of timing brings into focus the two sides of every birth, the giving and the receiving. Someone is birthing the dream and others are receiving it. Proper timing takes both into account.

Growing up in the home of a pastor can be unique. I can remember one of the first times I realized I was not being treated like other children. It was in the main hallway of the church my parents pastored in New Bedford, Massachusetts. A man with children my age stopped me and asked to meet with me. We stepped into a Sunday School room and sat down. I could not imagine what he wanted to talk about, but I was willing. He began to share with me some of the issues he was having with one of his children. I listened politely, but I was completely shocked when I realized that he was asking my advice on how he should address the issues. If my memory serves, I would have been about fourteen.

Today, I am the husband of a wonderful wife of twenty-one years. We have two incredible sons who are nineteen and sixteen. They are both strong believers, doing well in school, and volunteer in the church. I'm very proud of them both. I also pastor a great church, and questions on parenting are no longer a surprise to me. By this point in my life, I have experiential knowledge of parenting.

I can't remember all of what I said to that man, but I do recall saying, *"I am obviously too young to have children, but I'll tell you what my parents do with me."* Most people can see the problem here. There would come a time when I would be able to offer advice to a parent, but not as a fourteen-year-old. Sure, as a fairly reflective youth, I understood a few things and had an opinion about everything. I pray that those seeking my advice consulted with a few adults prior to taking action.

Forcing the vision artificially may seem to move you further faster, but it could also destroy you and damage those you influence.

When Jesus was fourteen, even He wasn't declaring Himself Savior. He was Savior at both fourteen and thirty years old, but at that age, He had not experienced certain things needed to begin that season of His life. Neither Jesus nor I were prepared to engage in the full destiny of our lives as teenagers.

You may be older than that, but your life could still be unprepared to conceive, carry, and birth what God has planned. Forcing the vision artificially may seem to move you further faster, but it could also destroy you and damage those you influence.

In the case of Jesus, He was never unprepared for His birth. As God made flesh, He would have lived a perfect life. It's more likely that the world was not yet ready for Him. That is the receiving element of this birthing process.

The High Price of Change

Years before Amazon was a household name, Kristy and I launched a web-based bookstore. The internet was just becoming widespread. Dial-up modems were causing phones to give a busy signal all across the fruited planes. We were living in California at the time and had developed relationships with several Christian authors. Money was tight and time was tighter. At some point, we established that if the internet could be used as a sales platform, an internet-based bookstore was possible. Kristy had just begun learning how to develop websites, so we spoke to several authors, built the site, and launched. We had one investor and one really big idea. We began pushing the site in every way we knew. We invested everything we had, but ultimately lost it all.

This was one of the lowest times of my life. I felt I had failed everyone. It was my job to sell the concept and get the books sales going. Not only had we lost our money, but also the money of the one investor who believed in our vision. That investor came to me one day not long after beginning the endeavor. I had opened the mail and there was his check with a letter. He wrote, *"You told me about your idea, and while I don't understand anything about the internet, I like what you said, and I believe in you."* The letter was signed *"Pawpaw."* My grandfather believed in me.

I called him and refused the check, but he demanded I accept. I told him I had no idea whether this would work and I could not put him at risk. He told me it was his money to risk and I was his grandson. If I lost it all but learned something from it – then the lesson was worth the investment. We deposited the check.

I was so upset I'd lost all of Pawpaw's money that I became physically ill. For months I avoided his calls or made them as short as possible. One day he addressed the issue directly, and we started to smooth things over. As time went on, I was able to allow our relationship to return to normal, but for years there was a fleeting thought of my failure that caused me to feel the pain, guilt, and shame over again.

This was my reality until I read the story of Jeff Bezos and Amazon. By this time Amazon was becoming the mammoth company we know today. Reading about an online bookstore becoming a billion-dollar company was, at first, quite disturbing to me, but I kept reading – and I'm glad I did. One fact, in particular, opened my heart to redemption. Mr. Bezos launched Amazon with several hundred thousand dollars and had over eight million dollars invested over the following year. Many millions followed those initial investments. In total, Amazon operated for six years before becoming profitable. That's how much money and time it took this new concept to become accepted.

I was redeemed – our idea was sound, and our work was good, but we were completely naive to the cultural changes necessary to make online purchasing acceptable. In short, the world was not ready for the idea, and we didn't have the capital needed to change culture. Amazon was able to push the shift and has risen to incredible success because of it.

If you've identified a dream locked up within you, but haven't yet experienced conception, one of two things are possible. First, you aren't ready yet to carry the weight of what you will give birth to. Second, the world isn't ready for your idea yet, and you don't have the capital to survive the shift needed in culture.

I encourage you to relax. Yes, that's hard to hear, and it might irritate you. That is normal, and it doesn't change the reality of timing. Conception will occur if you remain open, unified and patient.

Frustration rarely creates anything beautiful.

Before moving on, I want to speak to a segment of readers who have already birthed something great. Maybe you have written a song being sung by many, but it seems like it was the only song in you. You are afraid of being a *"one hit wonder."* Let me encourage you in two ways. First, becoming a *"one hit wonder"* is more than most will ever experience. While that doesn't help you write the next song, be grateful for that blessing. Frustration rarely creates anything beautiful.

I know one couple that, with their doctor's help, were able to trace their fertility issues to the stress created by repeatedly trying to conceive without success. Following that revelation, they stopped focusing on having a baby and went on a vacation.

To their surprise, they discovered they were expecting just a few weeks after returning home.

Relax and trust that the cycle continues and you will become fertile again.

The timing challenge is real, and it is not always yours to control. This is where faith comes in. You could choose to walk away from the dream God placed within you, or you could decide to force the timing forward and potentially hurt yourself and others. The best choice is to wait on the Lord. It is the only option that engages your faith and frees God to work His will in your life.

The old timers I grew up around used to say, *"God is never late nor is He early. He is always right on time."* I believe your story will read, *"When the right time had come, God empowered your dream, and it became a living thing within your life."*

CHAPTER 7

The Why

At this point, the need for conception has become under-stood. The breakdown of what can stop it from occurring has hopefully helped to bring clarity to some of the struggles you have experienced in birthing your destiny. I pray the Holy Spirit is working in you even now to define the vision God has placed within your life. I believe he wants you to do something wonderful!

We must turn now to the important question of *"Why?"* Why has God placed this new thing within you and why should you give birth to anything at all?

In 2009, author Simon Sinek released a great book titled, *"Start with Why: How Great Leaders Inspire Everyone to Take Action."* He suggests that there are two main ways to influence human behavior. While both manipulation and inspiration can produce results, inspiring people to action is more effective and beneficial. Inspiring people to act is more powerful than manipulation in the long term.

I usually begin by answering the *"why"* before I engage in the *"what,"* but not this time. The reason is simple. Most people hope to do more and be more than they currently are. Even if they don't express these feelings openly, they secretly hope for it. They pray that things will at some point align and reveal their true callings and potential. This hidden hope is why the stories of Cinderella and Beauty and the Beast have stood the test of time. It's why I believe most superheroes have a backstory involving a unique and absolutely unbelievable moment when their potential is unlocked and suddenly released into the world.

In these fantasies, extreme abilities come upon the character unexpectedly, and their release or use seems to be a natural part of the character's life. Due to circumstances beyond their control, great power is revealed. It's clear just taking a quick look at a few of the most well-known heroes of these stories.

Peter Parker is accidentally bitten by a radioactive spider. Instead of dying, he develops superpowers. Because of this accident, he becomes the only real hope of stopping the crime wave in New York City. While he battles with self-doubt and the fear that others will discover his true identity, Parker continues to swing into action and defeat villain after villain. He has captured the hearts and imagination of fans for generations.

> *Most people hope to do more and be more than they currently are.*

In Beauty and the Beast, Belle comes to the rescue of her father who had been captured by a fierce beast. The beast releases her father in exchange for Belle. What she didn't know was that the beast was really a handsome prince whose selfishness had resulted in a curse turning him into this beast. Unknowingly, Belle had become his last chance at becoming human again. She was able to look past his outward appearance and stand up to him when all others were afraid, so she won his heart and fell in love. Ultimately the Beast gives his life to save Belle which breaks the curse and heals him. Belle and her wealthy, handsome, humble, and caring prince are married and live happily ever after.

These stories unexpectedly empower the individual and typically launch them into the spotlight. Becoming someone worth admiring and doing great things are simply a byproduct of survival. This is fantasy, but many hope their life produces these results, and are usually disappointed. In real life, the release of positive potential is rarely sudden and involves a lot of intentionality and hard work.

Understanding *"why"* you are doing what you are doing empowers you during difficult times. When the *"what"* isn't enough, the *"why"* makes the difference.

Seeking Approval

The uniquely human reality is that a conception may not be *"right."* It is possible to conceive and birth something that will not bring happiness, fulfillment, or success into your life. It's even possible to birth something that will ultimately destroy you. The right conception will result in something that will bring lasting benefit to your life and the world.

It would be fantastic to think that everything conceived was wanted, but we know that this is false. Sometimes conception occurs with little to no thought put into the result. Other times it is simply a means to an end.

Scripture tells us the tragic story of Leah.[22] She was the first wife of Jacob, but not the wife that he loved. In that time, a marriage was more contractual than today. The groom would propose a deal to a father for his daughter's hand in marriage. Jacob had fallen in love with Rachel. Her father, Laban, agreed that Jacob could marry Rachel if he agreed to work for Laban for seven years. Jacob agreed.

Seven years later, Jacob was ready to marry Rachel, but then Laban switched Rachel for her older and less attractive sister, Leah. Because the wedding attire covered the bride completely, Jacob did not know he had married Leah until the next morning when they woke up together. He was furious.

Laban explained his actions by saying, *"Leah is the older daughter and should be married first. I'll give you Rachel in ex-*

change for another seven years of work, but allow Leah to be your only wife for one week." Jacob agreed.

Tragically, Leah was not loved as a wife should be. It was not her fault, but it was her reality.

Soon, Leah conceived and gave birth to a son. She named him Reuben. We get a glimpse into her heart by looking at the meaning of the name. Reuben means *"see a son."* The scripture records Leah saying, *"The Lord has noticed my misery, and now my husband will love me."*[23] Leah had conceived to win the love of Jacob.

I wish this didn't happen today, but it does. There are many women who feel that their marriage isn't strong, so they conceive to draw their husband's attention. This concept isn't acted out with the conception of children alone.

Launching a business to fulfill your father's dream will not bring you happiness or success. Planting a church to prove to others that you are a senior pastor will result in heartache, pain, and little joy. Inventing a new product just to prove you are as intelligent as your sibling will probably be a long-term failure.

Both men and women have taken on careers they don't enjoy hoping to make their parents proud. Some choose their school based on where their family went instead of where they dream of attending. Others marry the person their parents think is right while dreaming of someone different.

Launching a business to fulfill your father's dream will not bring you happiness or success. Planting a church to prove to others that you are a senior pastor will result in heartache, pain, and little joy. Inventing a new product just to prove you are as intelligent as your sibling will probably be a long-term failure.

Giving birth to gain the approval or love of another will not produce the offspring you are hoping for. Leah was happy to give

Jacob a son, but to Jacob it was a son of deception, not a son of promise. Over the years, Leah conceived many more sons with her husband while Rachel always struggled to conceive. This reality didn't change Leah's situation. Despite the children she conceived, she never became the focus of her husband's affections.

I've made this mistake. As a young preacher, I desired the approval of the elder ministers around me. At one point, a man I admired, who I'll call Bill, asked me to launch a new ministry. Kristy and I prayed and discussed the idea. We decided to hold off for one year to become financially stable before moving forward. A few days later I shared our thoughts with Bill. He immediately began urging me to launch now and not wait. It was a full-court press. Soon Bill called me saying, *"I've raised the money you need so you can go now."* Kristy and I agreed.

Eventually, Bill's promises fell through. He did half of what he promised and left us to scramble for the rest. For a time, our family struggled desperately to survive simply because we conceived something with the wrong partner.

Offspring birthed from deception can become a blessing in time, but this is not the *"why"* that produces the *"right"* baby for your life.

Seeking a Thrill

While attempting to gain love, affection, or praise by conceiving is a mistake, it is not the only negative reason to conceive. Some conceive because the process can be fun. There is a rush of adrenaline whenever first thinking about the new possibility. The rush continues each time a new barrier is crossed and the moment of conception approaches. Some become so attached to the experience of conception that they repeat the process constantly.

If this is your reality, you may find yourself always becoming excited about new ideas. Your excitement is so intense that it becomes contagious, so as you share these ideas with others they become excited too. You enjoy dreaming of what could be. The conversations reinforce your excitement, and soon you find yourself moving toward making the idea a reality. At some point you make the agreement, file the paperwork, and toast the beginning of a new life.

> *Our world is full of deadbeat dads. It is also full of serial conceivers – those who are always launching a new thing but never putting in the effort to see it grow.*

It is here that those who are in love with the act of conception will usually feel their excitement wane. As the process continues, they will pull back, second guess, and find fault, similar to a man who enjoys an intimate relationship with a lady, but disappears when she reveals she is pregnant. He enjoys the sex but doesn't want the responsibility of a long-term relationship and fatherhood. Our world is full of deadbeat dads. It is also full of serial conceivers – those who are always launching a new thing but never putting in the effort to see it grow.

This isn't a book on the promiscuous nature of humanity, but it bears mentioning that intimacy without unity can be a fun and exhilarating process. However, conception itself doesn't bring lasting joy. I know many incredible families who have adopted children from around the world. They have provided warm and nurturing homes for unwanted children. The circumstances varied, but the ultimate reality was the same. The child was born, the parent decided they did not want to or could not raise the child and released them to be adopted by someone else. This book is about being intentional with what you birth.

A few months ago, my wife was overly excited to show me our brand new potato peeler. She didn't need potato's peeled. She just wanted to show me the amazing peeler she had purchased. In reality, I don't care at all about potato peelers, but I do care about her. While watching her demonstrate the ease with which this newly designed peeler was getting the job done, I thought, *"This is a tool that I care little about, but it brings happiness to Kristy. This is an idea that someone brought from conception to birth and it will live on beyond them. It will make the world a better place one potato at a time."*

You may be birthing the next incredible potato peeler or the next Apple Inc. No matter what it is, make sure it's the right conception for your life. Make sure you know *"why"* you are conceiving this baby. The fact is, any fertile female can conceive with any fertile male. Conception is not a sign that the offspring is *"right."*

Right Partner, Right Reason

To conceive the right offspring, you must have the right partner.

Mary was open to conceiving. Remember, it was the only question she had. She was a virgin. Knowing that she was going to have a baby, it was only natural that she would wonder who her partner would be in this adventure.

Gabriel looked at her and said, *"...that Holy One who is to be born will be called the Son of God."* I don't believe Mary understood the mechanics of this statement at all, but she knew one thing for sure. If this child would be the Son of God – she had the right partner.

Finding the right partner is no small feat, but God can bring that right partner to you. The greatest reality is that God Himself desires to partner with you! He will partner with you in business, in creative pursuits, in planting churches, in missions efforts, in building a family, and in any other dream He has placed within your life. There is no God-designed destiny in which He is not desiring to partner with you.

We have looked at the wrong reasons for conception. Is there a right reason? Yes – to benefit the future. The value of the offspring must be the driving force of conception. What greater good will this offer the world? What higher cause will make the sacrifices of bringing this entity into the world worthwhile?

A time will come when owning a company, making a living, or being a composer will not be enough. Initially, just holding your baby will be the only reason necessary, but eventually, it will become your new normal. There must be a greater cause.

The angel Gabriel addressed this as he spoke to Joseph about God's plan. As I originally read this portion of the story, it seemed that he was saying, *"Joseph, this is why living through this experience with Mary is going to be worth it. '...she will have a son, and you are to name him Jesus, for he will save his people from their sins.'"*

Let's look at the options this simple phrase eliminates as reasons for conception. Jesus was not born to validate Mary, or to help Joseph. God's focus was not to give His Son a chance to shine. The singular focus of this conception was to offer freedom from sin to those God called His people.

What is your greater cause? What greater good will the product of your life bring?

In the early morning hours, when Joseph was up caring for a crying baby Jesus, he remembered the greater value and carried on. As Mary watched her son die on a cross, she could hold on to the greater cause. Having Jesus was not enough. The greater cause, however, was worth the price.

Your greater cause may be the sharing of earned knowledge. That is what drives me. Writing a book is a long and tedious process. In my mind, becoming an author isn't enough reason to go through this process. It's the idea that something new and extraordinary could be birthed from your life as a result of this effort that keeps me going. While writing, I keep imagining someone holding this book in their hands. I imagine hearing the words, *"I didn't know if I could do it, but I read this book, and it helped me."* I have a dream of a destiny being birthed, and that makes the effort worth the price!

What is your greater cause? What greater good will the product of your life bring? If you are partnered with God, then what you conceive will have a greater purpose than simple achievement. I pray your personal dreams concerning lifestyle, income, and influence are fully realized. I also pray that you never allow your *"why"* to be that small, and that - when all you hoped could become is now your new normal - the *"why"* of your life still stretches out before you.

More than two thousand years ago, in a little town called Nazareth, a young Jewish woman partnered with God to conceive something unique - the child Jesus. He lived, He died, and He was buried. His life was short, but His *"why"* has never ended. Thousands of years later, the *"why"* of the Father continues to mean as much as it did the day Gabriel stood before Mary. Conception occurred so that salvation could be offered. Today, it's offered in every language and in every nation. The words go something like this, *"Jesus, the Savior, was born to save you. Will you accept His salvation?"* Every time someone says, *"Yes,"* the *"why"* is validated all over again and the sacrifice is worth it.

CHAPTER 8

Yes or No

Nothing on Earth is more easily accomplished than halting the progression of a God-sized calling. It literally requires but one word: *"No."*

A few years ago, I became serious about my health. I changed my eating habits, started regularly exercising, and began losing weight. In time, I went from wearing size forty pants to fitting into the thirty-twos I was married in twenty years prior. It was not easy. It took work, discipline, and intentionality. I was feeling better, looking better, and had every intention of continuing the journey.

I was surprised one evening when Kristy said to me, *"I don't think you need to lose any more weight. I like that you are healthy, but I don't want you to be skinny."* This was not expected. Once I accepted that she thought I was getting too thin, I had a decision to make. Would I continue to work hard, exercise self-control, and lose weight or stop the process? She and I both knew that saying, *"No,"* to that process would be one of the easiest decisions ever made. It just took three words, *"Pass that cake."*

You can stop the conception of your destiny at any time. God gave you freewill. He will not force you to birth His plan. He will bring you into contact with the right people and you can refuse to accept the relationship. He will position you properly in the right situations and you can reject the opportunity. God will bring ideas into your mind and you can ignore them. The choice is yours.

Let's be clear, saying, *"Yes,"* is much harder than *"No."* Your situation may not be a good one, but remaining in what you know is easier than facing the unknown. I wish this wasn't so, but it is the human reality.

Change is Hard

The comfort of familiar surroundings and situations is powerful, so much so that it will cause us to remain in places we don't want to be and endure situations we would rather escape. Some people have a higher tolerance for change than others. From birth, my life has been one of many changes. Because my parents were missionaries and developing small churches, we moved often. I attended fifteen different elementary schools and junior highs. I then went to four different high schools. We have lived in many cities and many more houses. One of the side benefits to this life was developing of a high tolerance for change. It was the only life I knew, so it took me a long time to recognize that there was anything different about it. In fact, I was completely surprised when, as a young pastor, I witnessed someone choose to remain in a terrible situation instead of facing change.

I learned this terrible and valuable lesson from a lady I'll call Kate. She and I met in a hospital about fifteen years ago while I was praying for a member of our congregation. Kate was the roommate in the other bed. After I had prayed for the lady I was visiting, she asked if I'd pray for Kate. Of course I agreed. It was obvious that Kate had been in an accident of some kind. Almost every visible part of her body was bruised a different color from the healing process. One arm was in a cast.

I visited the room a few times, and eventually, Kate shared her story. She was living with her boyfriend, and they had gotten into a big fight. He had beaten her with a bat and this wasn't the first time. I prayed with her and made sure she had access to every service that would help her leave this abusive situation. The hospital staff encouraged her to seek help. I was certain that she would never return to him after what he had done. I was mistaken.

Kate had refused to press charges. A few days later, my incredulity increased when I learned that she had gone back home with him to complete her recovery. Her parting words to me were, *"He really does love me."*

Years later, I know that while Kate hated the situation she was in, it was also the one she understood. It is a truth I cannot understand, but I've now witnessed it enough times that I'm confident in that knowledge. This is the reality of many lives, and it isn't confined to abusive relationships.

There are many who are given opportunities to advance their lives yet choose to remain where they are. God provides the opportunity to conceive new life, but they are on permanent birth control, and so life remains the same.

One man, Jack, was a good husband and father but struggled to provide for his family. He took all the overtime the company would give him and even worked side jobs, but it never seemed to be enough. They were always just barely making ends meet. At church, we would often pray together that God would provide. Several times the church helped them meet unexpected bills and survive rough times.

One day, Jack told me that his boss wanted to have a meeting. He hadn't been told the subject and asked me to help him pray about it. I agreed, and a few days later, followed up with him to see how things had gone. Jack said, *"The meeting went great! They offered me a promotion. I'd be a manager which comes with a substantial raise in pay."* This was God at work. We had been praying and believing for something like this to happen, and He had answered!

I congratulated Jack and asked when he would be stepping into his new role. He replied, *"I turned down the offer."* I asked why, and he replied, *"I'd have to do paperwork. Sitting at a desk doing paperwork for two hours a day just isn't me."*

That was the day I realized that Jack was on permanent birth control. The opportunity was there. The conception of a new life was possible. Most of Jack's issues could have ended with this new position, but the fear of change was greater than the pain of staying the same. Jack blocked the conception of a new life with a simple *"no."*

Remaining in a painfully comfortable position is less risky than moving to a new position, but without change your future will reflect your past.

Why fear conception? Conception changes things. If you stay with what you know, you will be more comfortable in the short term, but you're eliminating any chance of positively impacting your future. Remaining in a painfully comfortable position is less risky than moving to a new position, but without change your future will reflect your past. Staying still is nice because it doesn't stretch you from your comfort zone or place you in uncertain situations, but without change your future will look just like your present. In the cases of Kate and Jack, their present realities would soon collapse under their own weight. Refusing to intentionally engage change reduces your ability to influence the direction of that change. Either way, change will occur.

There's a story of a lady who was laid off from her job. It was suggested that she go back to school and get her degree. She said, *"That's ridiculous! I'll be fifty years old before I graduate."* The answer was, *"You will be fifty years old anyway. At least this way you will be fifty and have a degree."*

You can't stop your life from changing. You can only determine how you will navigate that change. God has given you potential. He has given you the ability to dream, to plan, and to conceive. You can give birth to a whole new reality.

My name is not Gabriel, and I don't claim to be an angel, but this book could be God's voice speaking to you. He could be saying, *"I have a plan, and you have a big part to play. Will you say, 'yes,' and allow Me to do something beautiful through you?"*

If you agree, conception will occur. It may not be today, but soon a spark will ignite deep inside of you. New life will be birthed as the Holy Spirit begins to work within you. This process has no age limits or disqualifications. If you are willing, nothing can stop this miracle from occurring.

You can give birth to a whole new reality.

Mary said, *"Yes,"* and everything changed. That day a God-sized destiny was conceived. If your answer is, *"Yes,"* then you are releasing the Holy Spirit to begin a supernatural process in your life. You are ready for conception to occur. A new life will begin developing within you. Your future is shifting. Your destiny has begun to develop!

PART 2

Expectation

CHAPTER 9

Expectation Begins

This scene is common in today's dramas: The young lady is standing at the bathroom sink staring intently at the center of a small white piece of plastic. She's fixated on an opening in the plastic cover where a chemically sensitive strip of material is located. She has started a chemical process and is now anxiously awaiting the result. This young lady is about to find out if she is pregnant.

I remember standing with Kristy as we waited to see what the pregnancy test would reveal. We were planning to have a child. We were doing everything we could to conceive, but I was still nervous as I waited for the result. Yes, I wanted a child, but wanting something and actually having something are two very different things.

The thought of bringing a new life into the world was exciting. I looked forward to raising a child with Kristy. The process of conception leads to expectation. This test would reveal if we were living in a world of ideas or if we had transitioned into a world of expectation.

Don't expect what is not conceived. In a previous chapter, I shared the story of our dog Poe. She was miserable and almost frantic at times. She thought she was pregnant, but wasn't. This can happen in humans as well.

Years ago, I met a very sweet woman who joyfully informed me that she was having a baby. I congratulated her, and we parted ways. A little later, I learned that she was not pregnant but was a victim of mental illness. For years, she had been telling people that she was expecting a child. She was constantly expecting but had never conceived.

Wait for Conception

Be careful that you don't begin to expect something unconceived. I'll illustrate this point with a story about a man named Matt. If you met Matt, you would find him charming. He is fun to be around and is a great conversationalist. Within a short time, Matt would begin to dream with you about what the future could become. Matt is an excellent dreamer. He can paint a beautiful picture full of possibilities. He has enough knowledge to make a case for success no matter what the product may be. It is easy to want to jump in and make things happen with Matt. If you did, you may do everything necessary to conceive the dream. You may start looking for the signs that you are carrying a baby, but those signs would never come. Matt is on permanent birth control. Everything he begins ends before it is conceived and leaves those around him frustrated and confused.

Give conception time to work. Wait until you begin seeing its results before you move forward into expectation. Without conception, expectation is disappointing at best. On the other hand, what is conceived should be expected.

It is a surprising truth that some women deliver a baby without ever knowing they were pregnant.[24] When this occurs, for them it is a shocking revelation. A quick internet search will result in many stories of women from around the world who simply didn't know they were pregnant until the birth of their child. Some of them thought they were sick and delivered at home on the toilet.

Others felt so bad they visited a hospital and were shocked at the diagnosis. Every situation ends in a dramatic delivery. Confusion reigned as the unsuspecting parents tried to wrap their minds around their new reality. I remember reading how panicked they felt when they realized that their lives were not properly prepared for this delivery.

Knowing that God has placed something new and unique within you will drive you to conceive.

Knowing that God has placed something new and unique within you will drive you to conceive. Expectation should be your goal. If that conception is a business, then the development of that business should begin to occur deep within you. You must go through a time of expectation. For those who are not intentional about tracking this progress, the birth of their offspring comes as a surprise. This means that they haven't made proper preparations and the offspring suffers.

Are you tracking the cycle of your conception? If you took a spiritual pregnancy test right now, what would it reveal? Is there something growing and developing, soon to be revealed to the world?

Knowing that you have conceived is key to a healthy process. A woman who is not expecting, but feels sick every morning, is gaining weight, feels unusually hungry, and is increasingly emotional will probably believe something terrible is happening to her. The symptoms of pregnancy without expectation create fear and concern. Those same symptoms in an expectant woman bring the knowledge that everything is all right. Clarity can cause fear-inducing symptoms to become peaceful confirmations that progress is being made.

I believe there are people whose bellies have begun to swell. Spiritual and mental changes have begun to take place, and they are wondering what is going on. They have moved to the next stage, but because they don't recognize the shift, they are not expecting anything to change. You may be one of these people. I pray that you will recognize that you have moved from conception to expectation.

Mary conceived, and scripture tells us, *"He [Joseph] took with him Mary, to whom he was engaged, who was now expecting a child... while they were there, the time came for her baby to be born."* [25] By, *"time,"* Luke is referring to the moment when the child was ready to make His way into the waiting world. The word time is used instead of moment because the delivery was not occurring directly after conception. Mary conceived, but she wasn't handed a child. The child had to develop within her for nine months. After that, she would give birth. This in-between time is called the expectation.

Time to Respond

Expectation is the strong belief that something is going to happen. There are few initial signs, but the process makes everything clearer as time passes. Because of the knowledge that birth is coming, a response is demanded.

As a child, I participated in game nights at my parents' home. One of my favorite games was called Murder in the Dark. The players would all pick a paper out of a bowl indicating the part they would play. One would be a detective and one would be a murderer. The rest of the players would be possible victims.

Once everyone knew their role, we'd turn off the lights and the players would disperse through the house. At some point the *"murderer"* would choose a victim who would lay down on the ground. When the *"body"* was eventually discovered by another *"potential victim,"* they would scream. We'd turn the lights back on and everyone would assemble in the living room. The detective would then *"interrogate"* the survivors and eventually make an accusation. If they were right, new cards would be drawn and a new murderer would be on the loose. If they were wrong, the victim would remain on the couch, the lights would be turned off, and the game would resume.

I remember the excitement I felt as I crept through a dark house. As a kid, this was fun and exciting. The expectation of feeling the murderer grab me caused an adrenaline rush. My home was normally relaxing, but this game changed the environment. Walking down the hallway was no longer a boring event. While playing this game, a visit to a common place could result in becoming the next victim. Because of that possibility, expectations shifted. During the game, my whole body was ready to respond to a sudden threat. Expectations shape responses.

We act on current expectations - in the present. If you expected your roof to cave in on you right now, you would move quickly to escape the room. When someone doesn't act on their expectations, their expectation is weak at best. James tells us that, *"Just as the body is dead without breath, so also faith is dead without good works."*[26] Action is the breath of faith. Without action, faith is not viable. Your expectation of the present results in a response.

Expectations shape responses.

Actions are our response to present expectations, and plans are the response to future expectations. We plan for what we truly believe will occur. When a family realizes they are pregnant, plans are made. Sometimes it is nursery construction or redecorating. Other times it is establishing a college fund. Kristy and I were living in a church basement in the Chicago area while expecting Tyrian. We didn't have space for any more furniture or money for college. Even so, plans were still being made. I remember Kristy proudly pulling out the second drawer on the dresser next to our bed. She had removed the clothes and replaced them with a changing pad and blankets. Even in a cramped and unusual space, Kristy had prepared a place for the baby. This was good for the baby and it was good for Kristy. It wasn't much, but she was planning for what we expected.

A person who declares faith in something they are not acting on is simply a liar. There is an ulterior motive behind their declaration. True expectation always results in a response.

Expectation is not always easy, and most would rather skip this part altogether. Dreams are usually associated with what comes after expectations. Families share stories about holding their child for the first time, or seeing their first steps and hearing their first words. Dreams are not made up of snapshots of the process.

Expectation is a time of development. It is the process through which the conceived is held in a protected and nourishing environment until it is ready to be brought into the world. It is largely an internal, private process.

Conception gives an enjoyable *"high."* Beginning a new thing is exciting. Who wouldn't want to conceive and immediately enjoy the result? How incredible would it be to immediately hold a baby after conception? It would be wonderful to conceive a company then immediately live off its revenue, to conceive a ministry and instantly walk in its full anointing and reward.

The dreams of what could be drive conception. Movies cut from a loving couple kissing to them holding their newborn. Conception and the realization of the conceived are beautiful moments and the processes of expectation and delivery are often glossed over. This was true even for Mary.

Reading the biblical narrative, we see a brief mention of her meeting with her cousin Elizabeth. This mention established the connection between John the Baptist and Jesus necessary to fulfill the prophecy, but few other details are shared. Nine months of expectation certainly included more than one family visit, but we don't know about it.

Even today, our celebration of Mary and the revelation of Jesus do not focus on the time between conception and birth. We sing of the announcement of Gabriel and remember the silent night. We do not sing about pregnant Mary gaining weight, totally uncomfortable, and unable to buckle her own sandals.

Our conversations reveal our focus. We talk about the baby to be, but I haven't heard anyone share their excitement for stretch marks, or cooing over swollen ankles and midnight cravings. Why? Because these battle marks of expectation aren't included on the beautiful website and glossy flyer. They are, however, absolute realities in the process of birthing a destiny.

It is in the time of expectation that the greatest number of destinies die.

Immediately receiving the conceived would be wonderful, but it doesn't happen.

Expectation is a time of development. It is the process through which the conceived is held in a protected and nourishing environment until it is ready to be brought into the world. It is largely an internal, private process.

In this section of Noel, we will break down this process of expectation and the wonder it contains, but there will also be difficulties. It is in the time of expectation that the greatest number of destinies die.

The conception of a dream starts a natural process that's developed and matured by expectation. If left alone, the process will continue until birth. However, stopping it will cost the baby. In the case of a child, this loss is often emotional and difficult. One would think that the loss of a dream would be less traumatic, but often it is not. While we can't compare the death of an idea to the death of a child, the loss is real as is its impact.

Some who have lost what they believed to be their destiny have given up all hope, saying words like, *"I tried that once and it didn't work. I'll never do it again."* Nothing in life works perfectly every time. The difference between those whose lives are filled with purpose and a future and those who look forward to nothing and leave nothing behind is their willingness to try again.

Don't Stop Expecting

There are many reasons that prevent a vision from being carried to term, but the most tragic is when the process is stopped artificially, causing destiny to die. Stopping the process before conception is called birth control. Stopping a natural process after birth is called murder. Stopping a natural process during expectation is called abortion. I believe abortion is the greatest killer of the future.

Destiny is a big word.

Over the years, I've spoken to a number of women who have chosen to abort their pregnancy. Their reasons have been many and well thought out. I've also read the accusations of some in the pro-life movement saying that women use abortion as a method of birth control. If this is true, I've not met anyone who has. Abortion is a scary and invasive process. Those women I've known have described their choice as one of the most difficult decisions they have ever made – and one of their greatest regrets.

I am pro-life. I believe life begins at conception and the future deserves to live. However, I do not and will not vilify those who choose to abort. Instead, I'd like to offer some great reasons to allow the process to go full term. The truth is that many of the reasons to terminate a pregnancy make some sense. These include the inability to support a child, the end of the expectant mother's childhood, or the hardship of continuing in education while raising a baby. These reasons make sense until we realize we are talking about ending the life of a baby.

These reasons also apply to the process of delivering a destiny. Destiny is a big word. It conjures up big ideas and, when pondered, brings the weight of responsibility. Just as with the birth of a first child, it is common for those who have conceived to wonder how they are going to accomplish the goal. Are they ready to raise the child? How will they provide? Will they be a good parent? What about their life will change? All these questions are asked no matter what has been conceived.

Move Forward

Seven years ago, I was talking with someone about the concepts in this book and how they applied to their life. During the conversation, the man said, *"This needs to be a book. You should write a book."* I thanked him and went on about my life. About six months later, I talked it over with Kirsty. It was decided that I'd begin the process of writing.

I began by reading. I read about writing for a while until I thought I had an idea of what I was getting into. I then opened a Pages file *(we are a Mac family)* and began to type. I typed on and off for a long time but didn't get very far. I blamed time, structure, and many other things. The reality was I was afraid. It was clear that this effort was going to require a huge investment of resources. It is time consuming and heart wrenching. More than once, tears have rolled down my face as I typed stories of my parents and grandparents or the incredible sacrifices of my wife. I went into this process knowing that great effort would be exerted and dreaming of the hope one may find as they read the information presented. I also had no idea if anyone *(with the exception of my family and a few friends)* would care that this book had been written. Those questions caused me to stop writing.

For several years, I wrote nothing. Then our eldest son, Talon, presented me with a gift on Christmas Eve of 2016. It was a wrapped piece of paper with a name, a website, and a registration code. He had saved money all year and was trying to buy everyone gifts with his own money for the first time. He and Kristy had discussed the fact that I was again talking about writing this book. I told Kristy that I thought the time was right. They researched software that authors use and found Scrivener. Talon presented me with the opportunity to download the program. A few weeks later I did just that.

I pray that you will not allow fear to drive you to terminate your destiny.

Until then, the idea of writing a book was certainly conceived, but it was not being allowed to develop. The baby was inside me, but I was refusing to acknowledge it. Fear of change was keeping me from moving into the next part of the development process. I was aborting the process and killing what had been conceived.

I pray that you will not allow fear to drive you to terminate your destiny. At this moment, I'm writing chapter nine of Noel. I have a long way to go before I know the answers to my questions. What I do know is that I'd rather invest the effort than never know what my baby looks like. I believe God has placed this book within me and I'm determined to someday give birth to it. I'm no longer in the process of conception. I am starting to feel the baby bump. I'm becoming comfortable telling others that something is coming. I'm finally expecting.

Can you feel things beginning to shift within you? Can you sense that new life has begun? If you know these things are true, then you too are expecting. It's going to be an incredible process.

CHAPTER 10

Don't Rush the Process

I'm privileged to be a part of a church with a strong missions focus. One of our strategic partners is the Pregnancy Center of Greater Toledo. The center helps the pregnant, provides support after the child is born, and counsels post-abortive women. When the expectant mother arrives at the center, the caregivers are there to welcome her. They don't know her name yet, but they are ready to walk hand-in-hand with this often-frightened individual for at least the next nine to twelve months. Sometimes their support lasts even longer. Why would the center be ready to assist mothers past nine-months? It's because they know pregnancy is just the start of delivering a child into the world.

Delivering your destiny is not an overnight process. It is a process of processes. The completion of one process marks the beginning of the next. Nothing happens instantly. Everything develops over time and in a specific order. When something occurs out of order, everyone and everything is placed in danger.

Everyone has flaws. Lasting leaders eventually learn to recognize theirs and plan accordingly. If they don't, they will condemn themselves to consistently repeating the same mistakes. A repeated mistake that affects one person is bad enough. Mistakes made that affect hundreds, thousands, and even tens of thousands of people should not be made more than once. It took me too long to recognize one of my weaknesses. I struggle to allow processes to work.

Allow the Process

I'm driven by visions and impatient with the present. This impatience has been tempered by time and experience but is still intentionally kept in check. As a young church planter, I was constantly looking for those who would help build the church. When I discovered someone with potential, I'd work to engage them in what God was doing. This is where my flaw would kick into high gear. Too often I'd identify the potential in someone that they had not yet realized. It was clear as day to me. Because I could see the possibilities, I'd present them with the opportunity to lead. My passion and skill as a communicator would usually persuade them to take the leap into leadership. They would be promoted. At first, everything looked promising, but when the pressure of leading became real, they would begin to crumble.

I'd love to say that the fault was theirs, but it wasn't. Often, I was pushing them forward, persuading them to jump, and because of that, the fault lies with me. I would promote them too quickly and just as quickly they would flame out.

In the early days of church planting, a warm body was better than no body. Eventually, however, my lack of willingness to wait for the process to unfold became an obstacle for the organization I led. The struggle to manage good people placed poorly was overwhelming at times.

The worst part is that I know that some of those good people would have become great leaders had I allowed them to go through the right process. I'm not crying over spilt milk, but I am recognizing the price of my flaw. Usually, those promoted too quickly would hang on for a while then drift slowly away. I simply didn't allow the process of pregnancy to work. I delivered the baby too soon. They hurt, I hurt, and the organization I led hurt.

Expectation is your current stage and pregnancy is the process you are going through while waiting to deliver your destiny. Don't rush the process! The process of pregnancy affects both the conceived and the one who will deliver the baby. Both need the process to work for the right amount of time for a healthy offspring to be delivered.

What I'm about to explain may seem simple, but it's a critical component to the process. Pregnancy is the process during which the conceived becomes viable. The development of a child makes this easier to understand. Conception creates a zygote *(fertilized egg)*. In time, the zygote develops into a blastocyst. The blastocyst is a hollow ball of cells which develop into an embryo. This is the first stage of development that most recognize as an actual pregnancy. The embryo is attached to the wall of the woman's uterus where it will grow and develop.

Your destiny will appear to be mature long before it is capable of surviving on its own.

The consumer version of the medical informational manual published by Merck says, *"At this time, the embryo elongates, first suggesting a human shape. Shortly thereafter, the area that will become the brain and spinal cord (neural tube) begins to develop. The heart and major blood vessels begin to develop earlier--by about day 16. The heart begins to pump fluid through blood vessels by day 20, and the first red blood cells appear the next day. Blood vessels continue to develop in the embryo and placenta. Almost all organs are completely formed by about 10 weeks after fertilization (which equals 12 weeks of pregnancy). The exceptions are the brain and spinal cord, which continue to form and develop throughout pregnancy."* [27]

It is interesting that almost everything needed for a child to survive in the world has developed within the first ten weeks of fertilization. Think about the fact that a full-term pregnancy takes forty weeks. Even though the majority of the necessary parts are there, the baby must remain in the mother's womb otherwise it will die. It will die with a working heart. It will die with red blood cells moving through veins. It will die simply because enough time was not allowed for the formed organs to develop strength. The interesting reality is that the child often looks like it can survive outside the womb long before it's actually capable of doing so.

Destinies are no different. Your destiny will appear to be mature long before it is capable of surviving on its own. You will see its potential becoming clearer. Its life-giving properties will become operational. The structural elements will develop strength, gaining the ability to reach and to stand. As these elements become visible, the one carrying the baby becomes eager to see the dream realized. Previously, the challenge was conceiving the child, but that has shifted. Now the challenge is keeping the baby in check and allowing the process to work until it is capable of being self-sustaining.

There's No Rushing

In my experience, most people are tempted to rush the process to *"live the dream."* They want to hold the baby. They want to play their song for an audience. They want to read excerpts from their novel to anyone who will listen. Sadly, those who rush the process soon discover that a dream can quickly become a nightmare.

The process exists to develop something into a self-sustaining entity. Today, a premature baby can often be kept alive by modern medical technology, but even the most extreme efforts from the best doctors and hospitals in the world can fail to succeed at times. In the birthing of destiny, there are few examples of a rushed process turning out well. We could also fill volumes of books with examples of those who had a great idea, rushed the process, and failed to see the potential of their dream come to fruition.

Remember that the last organs to mature are the brain, spinal cord, and the lungs. These elements cannot be judged adequately from the outside but are absolutely critical to the child's ability to survive. The only way for those organs to develop properly is to allow the process to take its proper time.

The most critical elements to the survival of your destiny will usually be the last to mature.

The process needs time, not only for babies. The one delivering the child is also in a process. Today, medical technology and modern procedures have made it possible for a child to be removed from the mother at any point. If the mother is in danger a cesarean section, or C-section, can be done. This procedure allows the doctor to surgically enter the womb from the abdomen and remove the child. Today it is generally safe, quick, and common, but it has not always been available. During most of human history, childbirth was a leading cause of death in women.

One of the leading causes of death for destinies is the failure to allow the process of expectation to occur properly. Think about what would happen if a nine-month-old fetus was somehow instantly implanted into the womb of a woman. One moment she is not expecting, and the next moment her womb contains a fully developed fetus. At best, she would be in immense, unimaginable pain, and at worst she would die a terrible death. Why? Because her body was not able to go through the process of expectation. The changes that occur during expectation allow the one delivering the child to survive the process and enjoy the fruit of their lives.

Many dreams are realized only to destroy the one who bore it.

Paul was a gifted speaker and all-around good guy. Everyone liked him and loved when he spoke at church. At first, Paul was grateful each time his pastor would ask him to share. He would humbly accept the opportunity, spend time in study and prayer, and always honor his pastor. Eventually, however, things began to change. Soon he began asking for opportunities and becoming frustrated when they were not available. When people would ask when he was next scheduled to speak, Paul would complain that their pastor wasn't putting him on the schedule like he should. Eventually, Paul became critical of the pastor's ability to lead and often openly criticized his decisions. At each stage, his pastor would talk to him, try to guide him, and love him. Finally, Paul declared that he was starting his own church. He rounded up as many people as he could, and they launched their church.

Soon, Paul discovered that giving birth wasn't as easy as he thought it would be. He found that keeping an infant organization alive was much harder than he'd expected. The stress of the situation began affecting his marriage and then his health. Ultimately, Paul walked away from his dream a broken man. On the outside, he had everything he needed, but he had not internally gone through the development process. Don't be Paul... unless your name is, in fact, Paul... then don't be that Paul, be a better Paul.

Relax

As you develop the destiny within you, keep the process relaxed. Over time, the expectations of others combined with our own excitement can tempt any of us into trying to move things forward artificially. We see this mentality on display as businesses are launched too soon, books are written before experiences have gelled into understanding, families are started before the parents can support a new life, and churches are planted before motive and mission are aligned. If this describes you... STOP! Rushing forward toward delivery will put both your present and your future at risk!

I've counseled many married couples who were struggling. My first questions are always about their dating or courtship process. Too often I discover that they really didn't date much. The story usually includes a few dates over a few weeks. Those dates quickly led to physical intimacy. That physical intimacy led to moving in together and a prolonged engagement, often a child, then marriage. It's not surprising that they are having difficulties. Their relationship didn't allow for the process of expectation to occur.

Many single people have shared their frustration in finding the *"right"* person. When pressed, they've admitted they often become intimate with a *"good date"* within the first or second time of going out together. Soon, issues arise as fears develop over moving too fast and wondering how the future will look. They haven't accommodated the process of expectation.

In both cases, these people chose to ignore the process of expectation. They went from not knowing each other to physical intimacy in weeks. Spiritual, emotional, and psychological intimacy was never allowed to develop. The result was a relationship forced upon people who were not ready to give birth to anything. They had not given the process time to work.

This principle is easy to see in the development of a relationship, but it applies to the birthing of any destiny. When the process works, those involved can adjust over time to their new reality. Change is slow, and the process makes them better able to manage the development. It allows the participants to remain strong and their baby survives. It's a win, win!

Often, the desire for instant gratification wins out. It seems like tomorrow is forever away. It feels like nine months is a lifetime. It feels like you must make a move now or your window of opportunity will disappear forever. All those feelings are false. They are luring you into a quick fix that will create permanent problems. You need the process and your baby does too!

In the rest of this section, we will discover some of the changes that will occur in your life as your future begins taking shape. Carefully note the changes in your life. By paying attention to them, you will know when the time to deliver is upon you.

CHAPTER 11

Embracing Expectation

The astute reader has picked up that I've been fortunate to live in many places in my lifetime. At present, I'm living in my fourth country, sixth state, and thirty-second home. Today we are happily settled in Northwest Ohio, those days of moving hopefully behind us. Moving so often has negative realities. As a young boy, leaving friends was always difficult. Changing schools was tough. Before the days of Facebook, moving meant leaving and never speaking again. I'm thankful to those friends and schoolmates I've had over the years who have connected with me on social media. It also means the few remaining friends I have from childhood mean a great deal to me. Yes, there were negatives. The positive, however, is that change became my *"normal"* and has not derailed my life like it has for so many others. God has used our family in unique ways that may not have been possible had I not been familiar with the process of change.

When God is birthing something unique from your life, change is unavoidable. The focus is often on the changes that others must make to adjust to the new life that is developing within you. It is natural, and right, for you to begin assessing the relational and locational changes that are forming outside your life. The expecting parents usually begin child proofing long before the birth happens. Some begin assessing friends and activities with the wellbeing of their child in mind. When creating businesses, books, careers, and other non-biological entities, there are seminars, books, and messages focusing on creating right atmospheres. Experts will encourage you not to limit your potential with the perspectives and opinions of others. A quick browse through any book retailer will result in authors helping you negotiate the changing relational tides of life. I agree with many of them and find their encouragement helpful. We will look at some of those needs, but before we examine the changes that others must make, let's focus on the changes that must occur in you. I propose that these changes are more important than the external changes and more often overlooked.

When God is birthing something unique from your life, change is unavoidable.

A few nights, ago Kristy and I were blessed with an evening of relaxation. We chose to watch a few episodes of the BBC documentary, *"The Mekong River with Sue Perkins,"* on Netflix. The show focuses on Sue's journey up the Mekong River where she experiences the beautiful and unique cultures along its banks. Her travels took her through the country of Cambodia which was ruled by the vicious dictator Pol Pot and the Khmer Rouge from 1963 to 1981.

During Pol Pot's dictatorship, he was responsible for killing twenty-five percent of the population, or between 1.5 and 3 million people. They were buried in mass graves as he worked to establish and maintain absolute power while changing the direction of the nation. Looking at this horrible time in history, it is easy to forget that death was not the only story. Yes, many were dying, but others were being born. The internal processes continued to operate even as the external situation deteriorated. Those that focused solely on the external would have concluded that death was the only reality during the reign of the Khmer Rouge. History reveals that even while many were dying, the next generation was being born. When Pol Pot and the Khmer Rouge were defeated, the Cambodian people survived. Cambodia itself was badly damaged and is still recovering, but it did not die.

What does this reveal for your life? Your external circumstances cannot dictate what God is doing within you. As long as there is life, there will be destinies birthed. Resist focusing on the external alone, but recognize the internal changes that are occurring right now as your destiny develops.

> *Your external circumstances cannot dictate what God is doing within you.*

Recall the woman from the last chapter with a nine-month-old fetus suddenly implanted into her womb. At best she would be in terrible pain, and at worst she would die from the experience. She must have time to allow the process of pregnancy to change her body to accommodate the new life, both in utero and before delivery.

Change is Coming

I'm writing to those who know that something unique is within them. You know that you have moved from conception and are now expecting the delivering of your destiny. It is imperative that you recognize the changes that you are experiencing. They are natural and necessary for delivery. They are not intentional changes, but natural changes that occur along with the expectation process. While it is beautiful, it can also be difficult.

Planting Legacy Church in Kona, Hawaii was incredibly rewarding despite the difficulty. I must confess it was a tough assignment from the very beginning, but God was faithful in every stage. After years of consistent struggle, Legacy was strong. We had a good leadership team, we were stable in culture and attendance, and debt free. Life seemed like it should have been good, but surprisingly it wasn't.

Hawaii is a wonderful and unique place. It is unlike anywhere else on Earth. Kristy and I eventually learned to love and appreciate the nuances of *"living aloha,"* but at some point, we stopped enjoying them. Things that we found endearing were suddenly annoying. The beauty of living on a tropical island suddenly became smothering. Nothing had really changed, but everything seemed different.

Recognizing and navigating the personal changes in your life is key to birthing your destiny.

These were some of the most difficult months of my life. I wrestled with what these new realities meant. I prayed for wisdom and clarity which were slow coming. One day, while driving down Queen Ka'ahumanu Highway in Kona, the answer became clear: We had finished our job and were now ready to leave Hawaii. It took me another six months of prayer and thought before I said the first word to Kristy about leaving. She and I talked and prayed together for months before we were ready to begin the transition. That year prepared us properly for the transition. Today, we are healthy and so is the great church we gave birth to in 2006.

The shift in what we appreciated was one of many changes that occurred within us as part of the birthing process. It wasn't comfortable or fun, but when the time to push arrived, we were ready. You can be ready, too. Recognizing and navigating the personal changes in your life is key to birthing your destiny. Allow me to draw parallels between the expectation experience of delivering a child and that of delivering your destiny. Examine your life. Are you experiencing any of these symptoms of expectation? Don't be afraid, but be aware.

A Word of Caution

Before offering you these points to ponder, I want to be exceedingly clear on the potential danger of these next few pages. Birthing your destiny does not occur in a moment, but over a lifetime. For those who desire more in life, the rest of this chapter may trigger a response. Be careful and prayerful as you read through these pages. Everyone will have bad days, weeks, or months. If you are in a tough season, some of these points may connect with you. You may identify your experience and will have a desire to respond. A response could be a decision, an action, or the releasing of your imagination to run free. Doing so without proper consideration could destroy a life instead of birthing a destiny.

Consider my twenty-one-year marriage to Kristy. I've shared that included in those years were some very difficult seasons. I know that I love Kristy. I know God has blessed me in putting us together. Even so, the thoughts of separation and divorce were many during our first five years of marriage. I'm thankful that we didn't rush into a decision. I'm so glad we waited, prayed, and talked non-stop for several years and built our marriage! I can't imagine what not being married to this incredible woman would have meant for my life. I know, for sure, I'd not be living the life I am today.

If you are living and working on your destiny today, but going through a tough time, be slow in making any decisions. Recognize that Kristy and I spent a year praying, talking, and seeking counsel before any movement was made. Our transition from Kona took almost two years to complete, and in the end, everyone involved was stronger for it. While God can save anything, a quick decision and action would have destroyed Legacy and possibly limited our future. Take your time and let the process work!

Having said that, let's address the first change you will experience as you go through expectation: the interruption of normal cycles.

Normal cycles will be interrupted as you shift focuses. In physical pregnancy, the cycles of ovulation and menstruation are paused by fertilization. The cycles will continue in time, but until the birthing process is complete, they are paused.

In the birthing of destiny, a similar reality becomes apparent. One of the scariest moments of my ministry was when I recognized that I no longer had a vision for what was next for Legacy. From the time Kristy and I began dreaming of a life in Illinois, I'd always had a vision. Sometimes the vision was practical and achievable, and other times it required divine intervention, but it was always there. Once an element of the church came online, another would begin developing in my heart and mind. At some point, I recognized that I could no longer see *"next."* This didn't last for just a moment, but for over a year. My ability to see what was next was my greatest asset in leadership. It was what had helped us navigate tough times and overcome impossibilities. When that gift seemed to disappear, it became a secret I guarded carefully. It terrified me to think about others finding out about my lack of vision. I didn't know why this was happening or if my ability to *"see"* and subsequently lead was gone forever.

In a sense, I was like the lady looking at the plus sign on the pregnancy test wondering how her partner was going to respond to the news, knowing that everything was about to change and not knowing what those changes would mean. This shift became my greatest secret for over a year. It changed how I spoke to people. I didn't answer direct questions with a direct answer. I was consistently concerned about what was going on in my life and didn't know how to navigate the shift.

That's why I'm writing about this today. At first, I didn't understand what was going on, but I can help you address the shift with confidence. Maybe your great secret is that the thing that makes you good in your present reality seems to have disappeared. The cycle you have come to rely on - count on – has stopped. In fact, the very thing that made pregnancy possible in the first place no longer exists and it's freaking you out. You might have conceived, but it's just not showing yet.

Maybe your great secret is that the thing that makes you good in your present reality seems to have disappeared. The cycle you have come to rely on - count on – has stopped.

The danger here is that some abort the pregnancy out of fear. They believe they must have gotten off track somehow or messed up somewhere. The response is usually to race backward to the last place they understand to reconnect with that thing that helped them get them to where they are. I did. I spent months trying to figure out what I'd done wrong. I spent many hours in prayer repenting for sin or failure I couldn't identify. The reality was that I just needed to trust God's process for me.

I think of the disciples who returned to fishing after the death of Jesus. When I consider the situation, I see guys who followed Jesus for three and a half years who were racing back to the last thing they were doing before everything shifted. Jesus had found them fishing on the shores of the lake. Now that He was gone, they were returning to the last place they understood. This was not God's plan for them, but it was their response to their changing realities. Instead of waiting for further direction, they went back trying to reestablish the cycle they understood. I am hypothesizing here, but I imagine Peter thinking, *"Well, Jesus found me by the lake fishing. Maybe if I return to that place, He will find me again."* He then announced to the others, *"Guys, I'm going fishing. Y'all want to join me?"* [28]

Jesus did find them around the lake, but that was not His plan for them. He was changing their direction completely, but only time would reveal the full scope of the destiny they were carrying within them. It's almost like Jesus was quoting the brilliant Marshall Goldsmith, *"what got you here won't get you there."* [29]

Understanding a moment, casting a net, and bringing in a catch was one cycle the disciples understood. Most of them were commercial fishermen. This was also a cycle that would resume in time. Soon, Peter would stand up among his friends on the balcony of a second-floor room to address a gathered crowd. He would cast a net consisting of the declarations of the prophets woven together with the revelations of Jesus. That net would fall upon the ears of the crowd and capture them in the love of Christ. That day, thousands of people would be brought into the Kingdom of God and the cycle of casting and catching would resume in Peter's life. The cycle would resume, but the focus would be different as Peter and the rest of the disciples would fulfill Jesus's words, *"Follow me, and I will make you fishers of men."* [30]

It took me months of confusion and frustration to recognize what was occurring in my life. At first, I tried to artificially create vision. It wasn't successful. The result was a lot of work without much success. It was during this time the phrase, *"cost to benefit ratio"* was coined by Kristy and me. We got tired of working just to work and became intentional about the benefit of the work we were doing. Once I recognized the new reality, I stopped praying, planning, and preparing for what had been and began focusing on what would become. I wasn't certain about what was being birthed, but I knew it would look different than my present reality.

I pray that you recognize your reality far quicker than I did. If you recognize that your natural cycle has stopped, relax. Your cycle will continue after your baby is born. The focus will shift, but the gift God has given you will not be entirely removed from your life. Your ability to see, write, imagine, speak, sing, orchestrate, illustrate, and create will return as the process progresses in your life.

Your job right now is to fully embrace the expectation process. It will take time. Recognizing this will make it easier and more enjoyable, and you can begin looking for the signs indicating what's next for your life.

CHAPTER 12

7 Natural Changes

The interruption of natural cycles is the first change experienced during expectation, but it is not the only one. In this chapter, we will outline seven additional changes that occur with expectation. Remember, these are not changes that are chosen by the one expecting, but they are part of the natural process of giving birth to your destiny. Seeing them revealed in the life of an expectant mother confirms that the process of her pregnancy is moving along properly. If any of these changes failed to occur, the doctors would work hard to discover the reason.

This is a key revelation for your life. While many of the changes you will undergo will not be comfortable or easy, they are signs that God's process is working properly! Things are progressing normally and a day of celebration approaches. Recognizing the changes allows you to track your progress and properly address any issues.

Recall that in the last chapter I wrote that some of the wonderful and unique elements of *"living aloha"* became frustrating and irritating. Nothing had changed in my environment, but everything within me had shifted. I didn't recognize it at first, but I eventually understood that this was a natural change in the process. We received the same stimulus but experienced a different effect.

1. Same Stimulus; Different Effect

A lady we'll call Kate recognized the shift when she opened her bedroom door one morning and was greeted with the aroma of freshly brewed coffee. She loved coffee and usually enjoys the smell, but on that morning her stomach heaved. She ran to the bathroom and began throwing up. This was her introduction to morning sickness.

Morning sickness is the common term used to describe the nauseous feeling many women experience during the first trimester of pregnancy. It's a result of the increased hormones in the body and is often exacerbated by lower blood sugar levels. Most people aren't closely tracking their hormone or sugar levels, but they do know that what once made them happy now makes them sick.

Another example of *"same stimulus; different effect"* is the protective nature that begins to develop in the expectant mother. My wife, Kristy, has always been safety conscious, but her sensitivity to safety went to another level while expecting our sons. In those days, child-proofing made it difficult to open doors and access cabinetry. Long before the child was born, it was being protected from possible harm.

It is not always revealed in safety-related areas, but what was once considered acceptable often shifts as this change occurs in the expectant person. Hormones and blood sugar levels drive the changes in acceptable foods during natural pregnancy. The mother's nurturing instincts begin to emerge, making what was once acceptable no longer tolerable. These things are true in physical pregnancy as well as in the delivering of your destiny.

For those who aren't giving birth to a child, the process remains vital, but the drivers of that change differ. God is developing something beautiful in your life that, once birthed, will impact the world around you. However, without something pushing the shifts, nothing will change. As you move through the process, spiritual, emotional, and phycological responses to existing stimuli shift and spur the necessary changes.

A pastor speaks of how his life changed when the thought of a particular city brought tears to his eyes. He had been through that city many times without any reaction. It had just been a city like any other. He recognized the process of expectation in his life as he began developing emotional sensitivity to a city he never cared about before. That pastor, Chris Hodges, eventually planted a church in Birmingham, Alabama. Today, the Church of the Highlands is one of the largest churches in the United States and is still growing.

Henry Ford is known for changing the face of business as well as production. His assembly line made the automobile more cost efficient to manufacture and available to more people around the world, but the thought of manufacturing cars was not the driving force behind Mr. Ford's ideological shift. He had an idea that global consumerism could be a mechanism for peace. He believed that the wealth divide caused a societal division that could ultimately result in war. By making products less expensive and easier to access, he thought satisfaction would replace dissatisfaction and peace would arise. He became intensely committed to systematically lowering costs. This focus resulted in many technical and business innovations, including a new way to manufacture automobiles and the dealership franchising concept just to name a few.

Henry wasn't forced to risk his inheritance to give birth to something new, but the same stimuli that had always existed began having a different effect on him. This drove him to embrace the risk of change. What he birthed helped create the modern world we live in.

Without a change to our response to well-known stimuli, there would be no reason for you to embrace change. No reason to move forward in the process. Recognize the natural shift as things you have always processed in one way begin affecting you differently. What was previously acceptable becomes no longer tolerable as the process moves forward.

2. Changing Nutritional Needs

Expectation changes one's nutritional needs. Many women's eating habits shift during this time. A woman who is accepting medical care will begin taking prenatal vitamins to offset the nutrients being used to develop the child. Whether she is on vitamins or not, her body will let her know of its needs and desires.

When Kristy was expecting our first son, she developed a craving for Slim Jims. These are meat sticks that can be found in most gas stations and grocery stores. Kristy had never cared much for Slim Jims, but when she was expecting, she began to crave this snack.

I was sleeping peacefully very early one morning when I was suddenly awoken by her elbow. The elbow was quickly followed by her voice asking, *"Are you awake?"* I answered, *"I am now because you woke me up!"* She responded, *"I'm craving a Slim Jim."* I don't remember if I went to get her a Slim Jim that night or not. I do remember stopping at the grocery store the next day and buying her the largest pack of Slim Jims they sold. I sat them on the counter and said, *"Here is 150 Slim Jims. Now you don't have to wake me up."* I think she ate all of them. She hasn't eaten another Slim Jim since Talon's birth almost nineteen years ago.

Later, we learned that she was anemic. Her iron-deficiency was being recognized by her body causing her to crave Slim Jims. I wish she had craved steak.

Just as food provides our nutritional needs, our intake of information provides for our mental, emotional, and spiritual needs. Our world offers many ways to take in information. We can read, watch, and listen to information twenty-four hours a day and never even see a live person. Our further interaction with those we work and live with adds to our informational flood. If our intake provides our nutritional needs, then our health depends on what information we allow access to our lives.

While the expectant mother craves certain food and vitamins, she should also remove or restrict other items, including negative things like drugs and alcohol. There may be other items that must be removed depending on the health of the mother and child. Keeping track of changing nutritional needs is key to maintaining the health of both the mother and child.

Those expecting will discover their intake needs will shift as their destiny develops. Pay attention to what you are taking in. This process will cause your nutritional needs to change. At some point, you will probably begin feeling differently about what you are taking into your life. It could be a new sensitivity to content in movies, books, or TV shows. It could be a new aversion to certain types of conversations or attitudes. This may not be a new normal in your life, but it could be a change in your nutritional needs as you go through this process.

At the same time, you will begin consuming relevant information. I'm a reader. Novels by authors like Lee Child, Louis L'Amour, and John Grisham are like candy to my brain. During the times when I knew something new was developing within me, however, I read very little fiction. I craved biblical, business, and leadership knowledge. At one point, I realized I'd not read a fiction book in over two years. My nutritional needs had shifted. My new cravings were driven by the impending change in my life.

Your nutritional needs will change. Maintain balance in your life, but pay attention to new cravings. God is creating something new in you and it requires a shift.

3. Change in Weight

The changing nutritional needs are accompanied by increased appetite. Some of the weight gained by the expectant mother is the weight of the child itself. More of the weight, however, is usually due to the increased appetite. Because the child is pulling resources from the mother, both in utero and after birth, her body will demand more resources. When they can't be used immediately, she will store away the excess for future use. The storage system for resources results in gained weight. Our current culture is hyper-aware of weight. Some of this is an increased focus on health, but gaining weight isn't always negative. It is unhealthy for an expectant woman not to gain weight.

This is a more abstract concept and difficult to express, but I believe it's too important to pass up. As your destiny develops, your appetite for the nutrients needed to power your vision and your weight in knowledge and vision should increase. The increased weight allows you to exert abnormal amounts of energy without becoming depleted.

I was ravenous while plantings both churches. Every day I would read the scripture, listen to audio tapes, and read every book I could access. Often, I'd listen to a sermon or teaching many times in a row. I remember Kristy asking me, *"Haven't you heard this already? Didn't you understand it the first time?"* Yes, I'd heard and understood it, but I was hungry, and I wanted more of the nutrients that sermon or lesson was providing.

Your ability to gain and store resources will be a key in giving birth to a healthy destiny and keeping it healthy. If you don't have the resources to give, then your destiny can't receive them. Birthing a *"low birthweight"* destiny does not set it up for long-term success. A quick google search for *"risk of low birthweight"* will bring up thousands of articles and research papers outlining the many risks of a low birthweight baby. Your destiny will face many of its own challenges. Do all you can to reduce the number of hurdles it must overcome before it can stand strong on its own.

I remember meeting with an older man who had three grown sons - all of them older than I was. He did not attend our small church, but he'd asked for counsel on a referral from a friend. We talked for a while as I tried to help him navigate some personal issues. Nearing the end of our time together he paused, looked at me, then said, *"I asked you here, but I thought this was going to be a waste of time. What could a young man like you tell an old man like me? I've found you to be a man with wisdom far beyond your years."*

I was honored by his words, but I also knew that I was only able to draw from resources that had been put within me. He was gaining value from the weight I'd gained from years of devouring everything many pastors, teachers, and business and social leaders gave me to eat. He consumed my resources without depleting me because I'd gained the weight.

Delivering your destiny without gaining weight is a dangerous idea. Let the process of expectation work in your life. Take in the nutrients you need and gain the weight!

4. Change in Energy Levels

Expectation increases the draw of natural resources from the mother. Even with the increase in appetite and weight, many women experience reduced energy levels. The body is working to replace calories redirected to the developing baby. As the process of expectation progresses, the need for rest increases.

As your destiny gestates, energy levels will be impacted. I believe this is an often overlooked area of the process. The excitement of dreaming about what will become and the requirements of day to day existence make rest seem insignificant. The question most people ask is, *"How can I be more productive?"* This attitude leads to unanticipated problems.

In the second year of planting Legacy Church, we had the opportunity to move into a new location. Our church had outgrown the current facility, and the new building offered better visibility and more physical space. We were very excited. We were also working on a shoestring budget and couldn't afford the rent on both locations at the same time. We negotiated for a thirty-day window to move locations. The catch was that the new location was a brand new building. With the exception of two small bathrooms, the entire interior had to be built. Walls for classrooms and sanctuary space, painting, carpeting for the floors, all of it had to be ready to house the congregation within thirty days, and – believe you me – I am no builder.

Kristy and I worked in the building for thirty straight days. We would arrive at six AM, set up a plastic tent for the boys to sit under, and begin working. Incredible people from the church would arrive to help throughout the day after their normal work ended. One of the men, Trenton Johnson, had building experience. One day, he came to me and, with all the grace he could muster, asked, *"Pastor, do you know how a level works?"* He was tired of fixing the crooked walls I was constructing.

We worked until nearly midnight every night except Wednesdays and Sundays because of service. To say we were exhausted would be an understatement. We pushed hard and kept our exhaustion at bay by drinking every energy drink we could find. The building was complete enough to move into by thirty days, but it wasn't done. Our response was to keep working. I don't remember if it was our second or third week in the new facility, but I will never forget the experience. I was on the stage speaking when suddenly my vision went dark for a few seconds. It passed and I kept speaking. A few moments later, I became dizzy and my vision went dark again. I held onto the pulpit and continued giving the sermon. A few moments later, it happened a third time. This time I could barely remain standing.

I knew then that I was about to pass out, so I said, *"I don't know what is happening, but I am about to pass out. Someone help me to a chair and pray for me."* I stumbled to the front row and collapsed into one of the folding chairs beside my wife. A few moments later, I felt someone grab my hand and check my pulse. A man said, *"Don't worry, I'm a doctor."* That was my introduction to Dr. Jesse Broderson. The church was praying as he asked me questions. After hearing my story, he said, *"I think you are exhausted and dehydrated. You just need rest and fluids."*

The church was happy, and I was thankful yet embarrassed. I was thankful that God had provided a doctor to help me that day. It was Jesse and Shannon Broderson's first visit to the church. They have become lifelong friends. I was embarrassed because the issue was my own fault. I didn't recognize the toll the effort of birthing the vision was having on my body and it resulted in a completely avoidable problem.

I believe many expectant people make poor choices resulting in avoidable negative situations because they don't recognize their need for rest. I know leaders who have become exhausted by their efforts and began making poor life decisions as a result. My example was of physical energy levels, but emotional and spiritual energy levels are equally effected.

Great leaders who engaged in illegal, immoral, or simply stupid behavior can often be traced back to a variety of factors, including a lack of rest. This reality is intensified when expecting. Chronic weariness leads to frustration and self-medicating behavior. Rest is necessary.

Physical exhaustion demands physical rest. Emotional and spiritual exhaustion demand emotional and spiritual rest. Spiritual rest is found in times spent in God's presence in worship. Both Isaiah and Matthew wrote about the rest that can be found in developing a relationship with Jesus.[31] Personal experience has taught me that time spent in worship of my Savior is never wasted and always results in feeling refreshed and energized. Every expectant person must develop this area of their life to be fully prepared to give birth to healthy offspring and remain healthy themselves.

Emotional exhaustion leads to poor emotional decisions, so consistent emotional accountability is important. Find emotional rest by spending time alone or with those who are not an emotional drain on you. During this time of your life, friends who consistently need your emotional support should be given limited access. Friends who give you their emotional support should be held onto.

I find that picking up one of those fiction authors I mentioned earlier can bring emotional rest. Others find it while watching comedies or action movies. I'm not writing a book on how to rest – maybe for the next one - but highlighting the reality that during expectancy, your energy levels will change. Being aware and responsive to your changing needs will allow you to navigate the shift in a healthy manner.

5. Change in Handling Unnecessary Things

During every pregnancy, Kristy had a time of purging the house of unnecessary items. She has always been a *"throw it away because we never use it"* person. I'm a *"let's keep it because we may use it tomorrow"* person. During pregnancy, she threw away more than she collected. The boys had a nice assortment of onesies, but I could have shoved everything I owned into a bundle. Ok, that's not exactly accurate, but she did reduce the clutter in the house.

A physiological reality is that expectant women flush waste from their systems faster than normal. Their body is processing the needs of their own bodies and that of their child. Keeping everything clean becomes a bigger project. The larger the child becomes, the less room there is within the expectant mother for unnecessary items. This results in ladies excusing themselves to the restroom more and more frequently throughout the process.

Those expecting the birth of destiny will experience something similar. A growing restriction on what is allowable within the heart and mind of the individual becomes evident. Conversation will condense as focus narrows. Time spent on things off focus will begin to lessen.

Unmarried people and couples without children often remark on the lack of time couples with children have to engage in previously *"fun"* activities. Perhaps time is the issue, but more often the reality is that focus has shifted. Sure, a day with friends without the kids is fun every once in a while. The reality is, however, that people love their kids and enjoy spending time with them. The focus of their life has shifted.

The farther you travel on your journey, the more unnecessary things will be removed from your life. It may never be intentional, but it will occur. Eliminating the unnecessary creates the greatest amount of bandwidth possible for the development and birth of your vision, your destiny.

I encourage you to be aware of what is happening in you. Be careful not to close out those close to you. In my zeal to plant the church in Lombard, Illinois, I alienated my wife and children. It wasn't my plan, but it was my reality. We were building a church but losing our family. This was when the divorce conversations began. Thankfully, God helped me reestablish my priorities. I was called to birth a church, but before I was a pastor, I was a husband and father. It was my responsibility to manage the process that was working in my life.

As you mature and become comfortable in your new life, unnecessary things will begin to creep in again. During expectation, however, purging will be a natural part of the process.

6. Change in Elasticity

It sounds like I'm about to introduce a superpower. In a way I am. A woman begins releasing the hormone relaxin while she is expecting. Relaxin is well named because it causes the ligaments, joints, and muscles in the body to relax. This allows the pelvis to expand during childbirth, but it affects other parts of the body as well. Many women experience back pain as their muscles relax and can't hold them upright as usual. Most women become clumsy as pregnancy progresses. Her muscles aren't as responsive as they previously were. Some women's feet widen a full shoe size during pregnancy. Even the common complaint about heartburn is due to the muscles in the esophagus relaxing and not keeping the acid in the stomach from rising. During expectation, relaxin allows the body to stretch in ways that would cause damage at any other time.

A healthy process will increase elasticity while your destiny gestates. This may be demonstrated as increased patience or the willingness to negotiate certain elements of the vision. Sometimes, this is viewed as giving up or settling, but I see it differently. Just as the body relaxes to adjust for physical birth, so too will the framework of an idea to accommodate the delivery of a destiny.

I've already written that I knew we were leaving Kona long before it was made public. During the early days of that revelation, I was anxious and had major questions concerning how Kristy and the boys would respond. There was also one business reality I would not leave without addressing: debt. Both the church and our family were in a large amount of debt.

The major economic downturn of the early 2000s had taken a toll on the finances of the church. To remain open, we had taken on personal and corporate debt. Things had now stabilized, but I could not in good conscience leave the church in that state. This was something I spoke with God about in prayer often. According to our calculations, it would take a minimum of ten years for the debt to be paid. I knew we weren't going to be there for that long, and I was stressing about it.

Then it changed. One day I was stressed and the next day I wasn't. I recall praying one day, saying, *"God, if you want us to go, You have to make the way. I'm not stressed about it anymore."* What changed? Why did I go from being completely stressed to being calm about that situation? I believe the relaxin kicked in. I knew we were moving, but I wasn't trying to control the timeline anymore. I was allowing the process to proceed naturally.

It felt awkward. I was accustomed to being wound tight. Life on the edge of breaking was my normal, but that had shifted. It almost felt like I had given up, but internally the baby was still kicking.

Within the next year, God miraculously provided the ability to pay off the debt. It was awesome, but it felt like I was watching something occur that had already happened.

Relax in the process. If you feel yourself relaxing when it seems you should be tightening, let it happen. Your elasticity should increase to accommodate the new life within you.

7. Change in Comfort

Your comfort level will continue to decrease as your destiny progresses. Ask any woman in her eight or ninth month of pregnancy if she is ready to deliver and she will usually say, *"YES!"* In the early days of expectancy, she enjoyed feeling the changes in her body. When her child began to kick, a smile would light up her face. Then the kicks got harder, the baby grew heavier, her ankles began to swell, and then she couldn't bend over to tie her own shoes. Eventually, even lying in bed was no longer comfortable. She was enjoying being pregnant, but now she looks forward to the day her time of expectation will be complete.

Mary and Joseph were in Bethlehem when the scripture says, *"while they were there, the time came for her baby to be born."* [32] The process of expectation was complete in Mary's life. The closer you get to this moment, the more uncomfortable you will become.

In many ways we were happy in Hawaii. We loved that church and still do. The moment I feared the most was when we would tell the church what was happening. I knew I would stand before them and say, *"After much prayer and counsel, we have decided that our family will resign from pastoring Legacy Church and move to Houston, Texas."* This was going to be a moment that would rip my heart out. I'm a communicator by nature. Not talking about it to those we loved was terrible, but once said it would never be unsaid, so I waited to be certain of our direction. I dreaded the day I'd have to make the announcement.

The process progressed, however, and we became increasingly uncomfortable. To my complete surprise, when the day arrived, I was completely at peace. I realized that I was looking forward to making the announcement. As I stood before those incredible people, a feeling of relief swept over me. It was still hard, still emotional, and it still affected me deeply, but it wasn't the heart ripping experience I expected. In some ways I think that part had already happened. Now I knew it was time to move forward.

As you draw closer to delivering your destiny, you will become more uncomfortable. Don't fight it. Embrace it. It may not be time to push the baby out into the world, but that time is approaching quickly. Your lack of comfort is communicating a few things to you about the process.

First, it's revealing that your destiny is maturing. It is almost ready to move from your womb's protection into the harsh glare of the external world. If it is held within you too long, it will be too big to remove.

Second, your lack of comfort will motivate you to engage in the delivery process. I don't know if there are any other moments in a woman's life that combine wonder and fear like that of birthing a child. Historically, it was a leading cause of death among women, and the process of expectation causes her to become so uncomfortable that she welcomes the delivery.

The delivery of your destiny will be filled with both wonder and pain. This awareness grows the closer you get to that moment when the contractions begin forcing what is within you to emerge. This change in comfort brings the expectant person to the emotional, physical, and spiritual place of saying, *"I know what is coming will not be easy, but I can no longer stay here."*

I knew we were ready to leave Kona the moment Kristy looked at me through tear filled eyes and said, *"Micah, I thought this was forever. I don't know what the future holds for us, but I know we can no longer stay here. It wouldn't be good for the church or for us."* These were huge words from her. She had arrived at the place in the process where she was so uncomfortable that she was ready for change.

CHAPTER 13

You Can't Stay Here

Kristy said, *"I don't know what the future holds for us, but I know we can no longer stay here. It wouldn't be good for the church or for us."* She was right.

During pregnancy, the time will come when it is no longer good for the baby or the mother for the child to remain in the womb. The time of expectation must end and transition into the process of delivery. In physical pregnancy, several factors go into determining when this moment has arrived. In our family, it happened in completely different ways.

With our first son, Talon, Kristy developed gestational diabetes. Kristy is a small lady and Talon was a fairly large baby. So, the doctors watched Kristy closely as her time of expectation drew to a close. Eventually, it was decided that Kristy was not going to begin her delivery process soon enough, and her delay would cause danger to both her and the child. The doctors decided to induce labor. The decision wasn't made by Kristy and me, but by the professionals around us who understood the dangers involved. Thankfully, they also knew how to avoid those dangers.

Our second son, Tyrian, came into the world in an altogether different manner. Kristy had an uneventful pregnancy and during a routine doctor's appointment was informed that she was in labor. I suggested we drive to the hospital where she could get settled. I would then drive to the house to collect the necessary clothes and baby accessories. Going home meant traveling the Chicago highway during rush hour traffic.

Kristy disagreed, saying, *"No, let's go home first."* We did as she suggested and arrived at the hospital almost two hours later. We let the nurses know we had arrived, and they quickly ushered us into a room. Kristy's cervix was already dilated to seven centimeters. This meant Tyrian was about to make his entrance into the world. He was almost born on a Chicago area highway!

One expectancy ended as doctors moved the process forward. The other ended as the natural process moved things forward. In both cases the, time of expectation had to end and the delivery had to begin.

There are physical dangers associated with pregnancy, but the process continues. To those expecting a God-designed destiny, the danger is great. I wrote in chapter nine, *"It is in the time of expectation that the greatest number of destines die."* Why? Because there is nothing forcing you to accept your Noel moment.

It's Your Choice

During pregnancy, there are times when a woman experiences great comfort. While doing research for this book, I interviewed a number of women about their pregnancies. One woman in her second trimester said, *"This isn't bad. I could stay like this forever!"* She was full and content. She was far enough along that she felt safe and wasn't sick anymore. She wasn't so far along that she feared the delivery process. She wasn't uncomfortable in any way, so the desire for delivery didn't exist for her yet. Unfortunately, for her the choice of staying in her second trimester wasn't her's to make.

Nature doesn't allow a woman to pause the process. Though the doctor's induced labor for Kristy, nature would have done it for her eventually, even if certain factors increased the danger.

The reality is, delivery will occur. A mother can choose to abort the child or birth the child, but she can't choose to carry the child indefinitely.

This reality is not a factor in the birthing of your destiny. Nothing will force you to accept your Noel moment. You can choose to carry this destiny within you until death and never deliver it into the outside world. It's possible to choose this option, but it will not be good for you or for what you carry.

A person reading this while still at the beginning of their journey may be wondering how anyone could intentionally hold off the delivery of the destiny God has placed in them. You are so passionately excited about the idea of holding your baby that you can almost feel it! The desire doesn't change, but the realities of having a child begin to come into focus. The process shifts your mentality. What was a dream begins to look more like a reality and the dynamics change.

You can choose to carry this destiny within you until death and never deliver it into the outside world.

A few days ago, I listened to a new father speak about the shift in his life during the beginning of the ninth month of pregnancy. They had been given an exact delivery date because his child was going to be delivered through C-Section. He said, *"I was so happy until later that night. I walked by the nursery and was suddenly gripped by panic. I thought, 'What if I'm a terrible father? What if I lose my job? What if I drop the baby?' All kinds of crazy thoughts flooded my mind and I just started crying in fear."*

If he could have hit pause on the delivery process, he would have. I'm happy to say that everything went smoothly for this family, but these thoughts are not unique to him. The conception and expectation are the easiest portions of this process to control.

Before conception occurs, many people live in the world of what they are going to do. This world is populated by phrases like,

"I'm gonna..." followed amazing and ever-present plans. This is the world of unwritten books, world-changing companies that exist only in their minds, and life-altering inventions that have never been written down.

The bakery looks great in your mind. You visualize all the cute decor items that will be placed around the shop. You and your friends talk about each of the possible pastries you could offer to customers. The trials begin as you work to perfect recipes. You enjoy delivering your fresh baked goods to friends, family, and coworkers. You dream of the day you will be standing behind the counter as floods of customers stream through the doors excited to try your latest creation.

A fantasy is awesome because it lacks the combined weight of responsibility and consequence of reality.

At some point, you recognize that the dream is growing, so you take the mental exercise to the next level. Maybe you begin scouting for the right location. Months pass as you and your favorite realtor move in and out of storefront after storefront discussing the pros and cons of each.

As long as the bakery remains in the hypothetical world, hidden from examination by others and protected from the realities of the real world, it is a beautiful fantasy. We like fantasy. Fantasy can shift without consequence. A fantasy bakery can be red one moment and blue the next. A fantasy bakery can bring in enormous profits and easily expand while you spend a fantasy month in Paris. With a fantasy bakery, you have plenty of time to focus on your family and friends without any detrimental effects on your business. A fantasy is awesome because it lacks the combined weight of responsibility and consequence of reality.

Some people move to the next stage and allow conception to occur. They begin expecting with great gusto, but never move all the way to delivery. These folks end up living in the world of half-realized dreams. This is the land where half-written books live. It's the land of business licenses for thousands of companies littering the junk drawers of homes. The license exists, but a location doesn't. This is the place where ministries are declared, but never launched. It's the place where possibilities are stored, sometimes for years.

A vision has been planted within the womb, conception has taken place, and the vision has begun to grow. At some point, however, the carrier of the vision hit pause on the process. A pause can be a good thing, but if allowed to remain for too long, a pause will become a death. The world of half-realized dreams is the place where ideas die...and that's the problem.

I'm writing to people who know that God has placed something within them that needs to be birthed. A God-designed vision is percolating deep within you. It has been conceived and is now developing. God is creating something new and powerful through you. It's progressing toward the world. It is meant to be delivered, but it can't be delivered if you won't allow it.

What God placed inside of you was never meant to live there permanently. It was designed to move from conception to expectation and from expectation to delivery. It is not easy, but it is necessary. You can't live in the fantasy world and expect to make a difference!

The fantasy ends when contractions begin. Delivery marks the moment everything becomes real. This is a scary moment. It's the last stop before the outside world judges what's been hidden inside of you. It is unfortunate that many people hit pause on their dreams. The combined weight of responsibility and consequence looming before them prove too difficult to overcome.

Let me encourage you. God will equip you for what He has placed within you. Expectation has its beautiful moments, but it was designed to be a process experienced for a time. In Mary's life, the scripture records, *"...the time came for her baby to be born."*[33] It was time for her child Jesus to be born. She couldn't wait any longer.

PART 3

Delivery

CHAPTER 14

The Delivery

Your time to deliver will arrive. I pray that you understand that you can relax in the process. Mary knew when she was expecting, and she knew when the time came to give birth to her child. The directions were given. She allowed conception to take place. The unique circumstances of her day pushed her to travel from Nazareth to Bethlehem. Ultimately, she did exactly what the prophet Micah had said she would do by delivering the promised Messiah in the town of Bethlehem. At this point, however, we find Mary in a stable about to deliver her firstborn child whose Father was God. She was fulfilling her purpose in the grand plan of the Father. This was a part only one person could play.

God doesn't give vision without purpose. He placed a vision within your life because there is an important part for you to play in His plan. He designed you specifically for this purpose. You are His Mary in this moment. No one else could do what she was called to do, and no one can fill your place, either. Will you allow your days of expectation to be completed?

Too many have aborted the process and destroyed the baby before it could develop. Others have delivered the baby too soon. It is possible that jumpstarting the process will be necessary, but it would be the exception and never the rule. In most cases, impatience with the process drives the decision. Impatience moves people to force the child out into the world. It wasn't ready, and it died. Both actions destroy the child and are reasons for mourning.

God doesn't give vision without purpose.

Understand the process and allow the time for expectation to come to a close. Making the transition comes with challenges, but also opens new opportunities. A child that's always expected but never delivered cannot live out its potential. It will ultimately be as if it never existed at all. What a tragedy this would be! God has placed the seed of something unique within your life. To this point, it has grown and developed, but its potential has not yet been tapped. In the womb, it can't stretch its muscles and test its boundaries. Kept hidden from the world, it is unable to make its own impact. It needs to emerge. I believe that which is inside you has incredible potential!

Jacob and Stephanie Cousino have been blessed with a really cool boy named Deacon. At this moment, they are only a few months away from delivering their second son. Stephanie works in the church office, so I've been able to witness the progress of her pregnancy. A few days ago, I stopped by her desk to ask how she was doing. Knowing she is a generally optimistic person, I expected and received a positive answer. *"I'm doing great!"* We talked for a moment about her impending maternity leave, and I expressed how much we were going to miss her around the office. I concluded by saying, *"We are going to miss you, but we are so excited about meeting the new Cousino!"*

Stephanie laughed and responded, *"I can't wait to meet him, too. I'm excited to introduce him to everyone!"* Jacob and Stephanie are in the time of expectation. Deacon is already completely unique from anyone else on planet Earth, and their new child is going to be equally unique.

We haven't met him yet, but he could be a future president of the United States of America. He could be the scientist that discovers the cure for cancer. This unknown child could be the pastor who preaches the greatest sermon ever heard. He could be the greatest evangelist for Christ the world has ever seen. He could build the greatest business in history. He might be the first person to travel to another planet in our solar system. This unknown child could be anything, but he will only have the opportunity to change the world because they had the courage to give life to what was within them. They do not know how their son's story will end many years from now, but they do know that it is within their power alone to give him life.

The reason so many pause their expectation and never move forward into the delivery process is the fear of the unknown future.

The reason so many pause their expectation and never move forward into the delivery process is the fear of the unknown future. They don't know how the story will end. Neither did Mary.

The song *"Mary Did You Know"* was written by Mark Lowry and Buddy Greene and first recorded in 1991 by Michael English. Since then, it has been recorded by many artists across many genres. The song asks a question of a young Mary. *"Mary, did you really know who you were giving birth to? Did you know that He would be all that He was?"* The most powerful phrase in the song is delivered at the end of the chorus asking, *"Mary, did you know that when you kissed your little baby, you kissed the face of God?"*

I submit that Mary did not know. If she could have known what it would be like to watch her son whipped, crowned with thorns, and crucified on a cross thirty-three and a half years later, she may have backed away from the delivery. If she went just a little further in the timeline, however, her feelings would have shifted as she watched her resurrected son ascended into Heaven to sit at the right hand of His Father. He would then release the power of the Holy Spirit into the lives of the believers. Seeing that, Mary would have known it was worth it all.

You can't know the end of the story, but it will never have an ending without a beginning. It can't have a beginning without you. God's vision in your life has been conceived, it has developed and grown within you, and now it's time for your destiny to be delivered into the world!

C H A P T E R   1 5

The World Is Waiting

The internet-based company launched strong with a seemingly positive goal of bringing customers to retailers to provide lower pricing. Retailers contracted the internet company to sell their goods at a lower price per piece in exchange for greater volume. The customer benefiting from the lower costs would become a repeat user of the service. Reading this description, you may have arrived at the idea that I'm referencing the huge internet-based company Groupon. Your conclusion would be wrong. I'm writing about Letsbuyit.com.

Letsbuyit.com was launched in 1999 in Sweden. It went bankrupt in 2001 and was purchased by a German group and given a few more years of life before disappearing. Researching the company reveals many millions of dollars spent in sales and marketing. Letsbuyit.com built a great suite of offerings to entice users. Many of its strategies were similar to what the multi-billion-dollar company Groupon has leveraged into success. According to Business Insider writer Pascal-Emmanuel Gobry, *"For group buying to work online, it turns out, you need a number of things: a critical mass of people online, a critical mass of small businesses online, a critical mass of people willing to pay for stuff. None of those things were around."*[34]

Undoubtedly other contributing factors exist, but the most obvious reason Letsbuyit.com never became a household name was that it launched too soon. The founder, Swedish entrepreneur and venture capitalist Johan Magnus Staël von Holstein, recognized potential. He and his business partner, John Palmer, developed a strong enough case for the baby's birth that they secured many millions in capital investment. The baby, however, was never able to survive outside the womb.

It seemed to have everything it needed to succeed, except time. The internet had simply not gained enough momentum in population or as a place of commerce. It was a great idea that was not yet ready to be born. Had its delivery occurred in September of 2008 instead of 1999, it would probably have been the Groupon of our day. Johan and John have gone on to other successes, but they were not able to live out the potential that they saw in the child they delivered too soon.

Proper Timing

Visionaries and deliverers of destiny often see possibilities before others. Believe me, I understand. In chapter six, I shared how Kristy and I attempted to give birth to an internet company in the late 90s that looked a lot like Amazon. We invested everything we had, and much that we didn't, and it went nowhere.

I've spent a lot of time and effort writing this book, encouraging you to take your time in the process. I've warned you about choosing the wrong partner when conceiving your destiny. I've repeatedly referenced the need for patience as the expectation unfolds. For some, that has been frustrating. My caution is intentional because I know what it means to birth something into the world only to fight for its survival.

Few things are more tragic than experiencing the excitement of a birth turn into a struggle for survival. Numerous parents have had this experience. The call goes out to friends and family that the long-awaited baby is arriving. People gather at the appointed places or wait by the phone to hear that everything has gone well. As a pastor, I have received the call saying, *"Pastor, our child has been born, but there is another problem."*

The story of Bill and Sue comes to mind. The expectation went well until the eighth month when Sue was placed on bedrest. That did not prevent her from going into labor. Their son, Grayson, was born in the morning. He was handsome, but he wasn't ready for the outside world. The only thing wrong with him was that he was born too early.

Bill and Sue spent weeks with him in the hospital as he fought for his life. The tears that fell could have filled a lake, and prayers became common among the family and friends as everyone did all they could to help. What others were going through was minimal compared to the pain of Bill and Sue. They were strong in faith, and for each other, but as the waiting continued, the story of their struggle was written on their faces. Bill would work all day then sit with his wife and son at the hospital. Our visits were full of words of faith and belief, but the weight of the situation was palpable.

It is possible for a destiny delivered too soon to survive, but it increases the pain many times over.

Through the diligent efforts of the medical staff and the grace of God, Grayson is a strong six-year-old today. He has overcome every difficulty and is thriving.

It is possible for a destiny delivered too soon to survive, but it increases the pain many times over. Fortunately, there is nothing forcing you to deliver your destiny too soon. Patience will ensure your child will be ready for the world. When the time is right, however, labor begins.

Every step of this process has led us to this moment. We have walked with Mary during arguably the greatest journey of her life. We listened to the words of the angel Gabriel and heard Mary's response. The transition from conception to expectation seemed simple, but it highlighted new issues to wrestle as her journey to deliver her destiny unfolded. Ultimately, Mary and Joseph made their way from Nazareth to Bethlehem, and the scripture describes the moment in an almost blasé manner, *"And while they were there, the time came for her baby to be born. She gave birth to her firstborn son."* [35]

Transitions

This description sounds so easy, like Mary was bringing a cake from the kitchen or a buying dress from the store. It seems to downplay what Mary went through, but that's not its intention. The focus of the scripture is the birth of the Savior. Jesus' birth was the result of Mary's process, so the specific details aren't necessary for the point to be made. For our purpose, however, the details of her delivery process need to be broken down. We desire to understand what occurred as Mary's destiny transitioned from her womb and into the world.

It would seem that after waiting for the process of conception to complete, then enduring the forty-week process of expectation, the delivery would be quick. This is not always the case.

The DailyMail reported the incredible story of the Joanna Krzysztonek, whose labor lasted seventy-five days![36] Pregnant with triplets, she had gone into labor too soon. Her first child delivered could not survive. In the effort to save the other two children, doctors used drugs that reduced contractions. They also had Joanna lay almost upside down for over ten weeks. Thankfully, she and her two surviving children are healthy today.

We have written repeatedly that your destiny is a process of processes. That fact remains true in delivery. As you shift from expectation to delivery, one process will give way to another. Learning to recognize the shift will cause the experience to be easier and less stressful.

Some become frustrated that after months and sometimes years of waiting, there is yet another process. The thought is usually something like, *"After all I've been through, I don't want to wait anymore!"* While this is completely understandable, it doesn't change your current reality.

Stated simply, the delivery is the process that moves what is inside of you outside of you. It is the final internal step in the process of delivering your destiny. It is the first external step your baby will make. Congratulations! Your baby is going public!

Overall, pregnancy is a woman's most life-threatening natural process. Within this process of processes, delivery is the most dangerous. Research into the reasons behind the birthing process's danger reveals an incredibly wide range of factors. Complications arising from dangerously high blood pressure *(preeclampsia)*, obesity, quality of medical care, ruptures of tissue, and the increasing age of pregnant women. These are just a few of the variables that have been identified in the research published by the World Health Organization and the 2016 Obstetrics & Gynecology study authored by research professor Marian MacDorman of the University of Maryland.

Stated simply, the delivery is the process that moves what is inside of you outside of you. It is the final internal step in the process of delivering your destiny.

For our purposes, I'd like to point out one overarching truth about the delivery process. In the hours it takes to deliver a child, a woman's body is stretched to its maximum. The pressure from the muscles naturally pushes the child toward an exit that's entirely too small. The stretching of the skin and uterus has occurred over nine months. In delivery, the opening and stretching of new organs will occur in hours if everything goes well. In every way, this is an arduous process that gives every opportunity for the body to give way to the pressure. The only way to handle it is to relax and trust the process.

Trust the Process

I like roller coasters, but I haven't always liked them. For most of my childhood, I avoided them completely. I gave many reasons for my avoidance, but the reality was that I was afraid. One summer, our youth group traveled to King's Dominion Amusement Park in Virginia. I was excited until we arrived. Somehow, I'd overlooked the fact that the park was known for its incredible coasters!

Because I was traveling with a group of friends, I went on a few of the smaller coasters without comment. About halfway through the day, we rounded the corner and there before us stood the Shockwave. I'd been hearing about this ride all day. It was a coaster that included one loop where the riders were completely upside down! My careful planning of our path had kept us clear of that ride until then, but those plans hadn't worked, and the decision now was before us.

I remember being asked if I was willing to ride the Shock-wave. I said, *"Absolutely not!"* I remember that we walked by it several times that day and discussed the possibility of riding. I can't remember every detail, but at some point, I found myself standing in line!

The line was long, so after a while I began to relax. Our group joked about the people screaming. We told stories, most of which were lies, about all the terrifying rides we had all been on in our whole twelve or thirteen years on the planet. We were determined to ride the Wave and survive.

I've forgotten many details of this story over the years, but I'll never forget the feeling in my stomach as I stepped onto the deck of the Shockwave. I was looking at yellow over-the-shoulder bars hanging over a small yellow bicycle seat that protruded from a row of blue posts. That's what I saw. What I felt was terror. My stomach was in knots, and I was certain I was going to throw up.

My sense of self-preservation caused me to frustrate the minimum wage teenage employee by asking questions about how the safety protocols worked. I don't think he understood the word *"protocol,"* but talked through how to harness myself in. He explained that the seat was there in case someone passed out from the G-force or just fainted. That made me feel a lot better! He concluded by insisting that no one had died on the ride in his long six-week career as its caretaker.

I considered walking right across the deck and onto the exit ramp, but at the urging of my friends, I strapped in for the ride. As I locked myself into the harness and the coaster began moving forward, I knew I was in a process I couldn't change and suddenly relaxed. It completely surprised me. I became so interested in my sudden change of state that I almost missed the sudden drop, the upside-down loop, the quick uphill that became a speed-building corkscrew turn, the gentle turn into the station, and the sudden shrieking of brakes. One hundred and twenty-seconds after locking in, I unstrapped myself from the ride and announced, *"I wasn't afraid."* We rode the Shockwave three more times that day. Each time I enjoyed it more.

Today, I enjoy roller coasters. I still feel tension just before we take off, but I'm able to relax in the process of being hurtled down the track at high speed.

I shared that story because it reminded me of how I felt the day our family boarded the flight to Hawaii to plant a church. Our home was sold, our goodbyes were said, and all of our belongings were in a forty-foot container on a ship crossing the Pacific, but hearing the click of the airplane seatbelt brought the same sense of calm as it did on the Shockwave years before. I knew I was in a process I couldn't change. I relaxed. Today I can testify that I survived the process.

Relaxing during delivery is imperative because it is unlike anything you have experienced before. The process changes you forever. It will stretch you beyond your known capacity. It will mark your life with impressions that will never be removed. It will cause pain unique to anything you've experienced before. It is also the only way to manifest the destiny that God has placed within you.

This is Going to Hurt

This pain is often tough to overcome. I believe it is because so many natural processes teach us that pain is the signal that something's wrong. It seems counter intuitive that pain would be a sign of something going right. Pain occurs in delivery both when things are right and when they are wrong.

Anyone doing something great, birthing something great, will experience pain even when everything is going right.

This is unique in the modern world. Pain management has become such a normal part of life. Many women today feel relatively little pain in childbirth compared to years ago. The scenes in movies depicting past childbirths reveal a sweating, screaming woman lying in a bed. Her contractions are being announced by her cries of pain. She is being told to push by those huddled around her. In the scene, there is usually a worried husband pacing in a nearby hallway or room. His concern grows as the screams of the woman he loves intensify. When she falls silent, he waits fretfully for the midwife to inform him whether his wife is alive.

That is not the experience today. The birthing process now features more pictures than screams. Kristy received epidural shots when delivering both of our children. We talked and laughed together as the monitors showed when the contractions were occurring. She felt no pain. It's an entirely different reality, so it's no wonder that so many think there isn't a price to pay in delivering your destiny.

Many believe that *"if it is meant to be, it won't hurt."* I'm afraid that this is a life destined to be small and insignificant. Anyone doing something great, birthing something great, will experience pain even when everything is going right. The reason for the pain is simple. The processes of conception and expectation produce a destiny bigger than your natural capacity to bring forth, and it must be strong enough to survive. Pushing it out into the world requires an expansion you've never experienced before, and which can't be duplicated artificially. The process of delivery is meant to be that way.

Jesus did the right thing, lived a right life, and it led Him directly to the right cross.

Jesus sets a great example of this reality. The cross was meant to be. Scripture describes Jesus as being the Lamb slain from the foundations of the world.[37] This means that God knew what was going to occur on Earth and His plan was settled. Jesus would live a perfect life and then be crucified on the cross to pay the price for all of humanity's sin. This plan was established before the world was created. Jesus did the right thing, lived a right life, and it led Him directly to the right cross. We read, *"looking unto Jesus, the author and finisher of our faith, who for the joy that was set before Him endured the cross, despising the shame, and has sat down at the right hand of the throne of God."* [38] Jesus chose the cross knowing that the reward outvalued the cost.

Stop asking the question, *"How do I avoid pain?"* Instead ask, *"Which cross is the right cross to bear?"*

The Price of Destiny

A woman pays a price for bringing a child into the world. Even if modern medicine can mute the pain of delivery for a moment, the pain still exists. There is a price to pay for birthing your destiny. The process changes you in ways you may not expect.

It changes your shape. A woman's body is permanently altered by pregnancy. Some woman find that they never again fit in what they used to wear. Many are frustrated or embarrassed by the stretch marks. Most work hard to return to the level of muscular fitness they enjoyed in their lower belly before pregnancy.

I write to mothers who have experienced changes in their bodies and struggle with their self-image. You have delivered the next generation to this world. You have endured the process and provided a future. You are worthy of honor! When you feel negative about the marks you bear, remember the little feet kicking in your womb. Remember the tiny hand moving within you. Remember that those marks are valuable. They were earned, not given. Remember that the price paid was worth it. Don't be ashamed of yourself, but celebrate your success. I celebrate you!

Selfish people don't give birth to destinies.

To those beginning the process of delivering the future, there is a price to pay, but it will be worth it. Ultimately it will bless you, but since pain comes before the blessing, many never deliver their God-designed destiny.

Selfish people don't give birth to destinies. I'm not referring to those who desire children but are unable to conceive. The selfish are those who have the ability to bring something beneficial into the world but refuse to do so. To them, the process simply costs too much. It would take too much from them and they are unwilling to give.

One morning, during the fall of 2016, Kristy and I were talking and praying about our move from the Houston area. We didn't yet know where we were going, but our senior pastors *(Brett Jones & Scott Jones)* were working with us and we knew the process was concluding. We believed that our move would be to pastor an existing church, but in the conversation, an alternative came up. One of us asked the question, *"What if God directs us to plant a church again? What would we say?"* I really didn't want to plant another church and at the same time couldn't in good conscience tell God, *"No!"* That day, Kristy and I decided that, *"Yes"* was the only good answer. No matter what God called us to do, *"Yes"* was the only answer we could give.

I've rarely been prouder of Kristy than I was that day. Birthing Legacy was painful. It was followed by more pain as we released the church to grow and develop without us. Less than three years away from some of the greatest pain of her life, Kristy was willing to say *"yes"* again.

Selfish people don't give birth to destinies while the strong embrace the process. They endure the pain knowing the value of the reward will be greater than the pain of the cost!

You have clicked the seatbelt on a miraculous process! Relax! It is time to deliver what God has formed within you. The world is waiting.

CHAPTER 16

Stage 1

There will come a moment when the expectant person recognizes that something has changed. Spiritually and emotionally, they may have been prepared for the delivery to take place for some time. This delivery begins when physical shifts take place, and expectation ends when the mother begins to physically move the baby into the world.

I've heard many people say things like, *"he just didn't want to join the outside world"* or, *"she couldn't wait to see everyone"* when talking about the speed of labor. The comments are cute but inaccurate. I've seen no evidence stating that the child has any impact on when the mother's body begins to transition them to the outside world.

You know that you are engaged in a process of processes. That's why it doesn't shock you to hear that there are three stages of labor. Recognize the signs and take your time. You are preparing to introduce something, someone, new into the world.

The first stage is defined as early labor. During this time, the mother is positioning the child properly. I know the feeling of being moved without choice. When I was growing up, my mother would often say, *"It's a beautiful day! Why don't you go outside and play?"* Her *"question"* was often accompanied by a hand on my shoulder guiding me to the door. Her approach was soft and calm, but I understood that her question was rhetorical. There was only one answer. Mom was transitioning me from inside the house to outside the house, and she was firmly in control.

While birthing your destiny, you are in the driver's seat. No one can force you to deliver. Neither can anyone stop you from going into labor. You have complete control. This is important to understand because the way your destiny is introduced into the new environment has a great impact on how it becomes established.

Introducing Your Destiny

Tim and Gretchen had been dating for six months when Tim asked her to officially be his girlfriend. They were getting next level. Gretchen agreed and they became a happy couple. One Friday, Tim invited Gretchen to his parent's home for dinner. She agreed, but since it was her first time to meet his parents, she was a little nervous. Her nervousness went to new heights when Tim introduced her to his parents as his *"friend from the school."* Until then she thought she understood her place within the group. She thought she was Tim's girlfriend, but now she was completely uncertain. The parents were equally thrown. How do you treat a *"friend from school"* who you thought was your son's girlfriend?

Tim was birthing a new relationship into the world, but his introduction, the moment of positioning, was flawed. He was defining how his parents would see Gretchen and how she would define her own position. No one else could be blamed for the uncomfortable nature of dinner that night. He couldn't point the finger of accusation at anyone else as he tried to explain himself to Gretchen. Tim was in control of the delivery of the relationship, and boy did he mess it up.

You are in control of the labor process. You set the tempo. If you are patient and methodical, the delivery of your destiny will be an incredible moment. If you hurry to the conclusion, you will lack the benefit of proper positioning.

Early Signs

The effacement and dilation of the cervix is one of the first clear signs of early labor. For the biologically uncertain, the cervix is the area of the uterus that opens. This allows for the seed and egg to meet and for the natural cleansing cycles to occur. After conception, the cervix is closed or plugged for the protection of the child. It's during early labor that the cervix begins to expand, allowing the child to pass into the birth canal.

The non-biological dilation process expands previously closed off corridors, and dilation opens previously blocked opportunities.

In chapter five, I summarized the story of how Legacy Church began. Our friend we'll call Joe had launched a church in Kona, and we had every intention of planting one in Hilo. Our goal was to hold off launching the church for one year while we established our life on the Big Island. We did not realize that God had other plans.

While our plans were being lived out, situations in Joe's life were preparing his family to transition back to the mainland. When Joe began talking to us about his thoughts, we knew that something unique was going on. A door that was previously closed was beginning to open. Dilation was occurring.

For you, this could look like a sales region opening in your company, or a house you have been admiring suddenly being put on the market. Your effacement and dilation story could include a relationship with an agent or publisher that connects with the vision you have been holding. Your process will be unique. The common reality is that opportunity for your destiny to flourish will present itself.

The typical question that arises is, *"Why now? I've been carrying this vision for nine months. Why is the door opening now?"*

At that point in my life, I was feeling like a failure. The church we launched in Lombard, Illinois didn't go as planned. The only thing keeping me moving forward was the knowledge that God was birthing something out of me. It had not happened in Illinois, but here was a new opening. Why now? The answer was simple. I was ready. What was in me was also ready to emerge.

God guides the steps of His children. He opens doors at the right times and in the right places.

Until delivery, every part of this process has been designed to provide maximum protection to the child while it gestates. Now, it is ready to move into the world. The obstacles must be removed for that to occur. Doors must be opened. Dilation must take place.

As a Christian, I believe God guides the steps of His children. He opens doors at the right times and in the right places. If you are not a believer, I pray you become one today. You can have an incredible life without knowing Christ, but it will always be better with Him leading the way.

Dilation does not occur alone but is usually accompanied by small, infrequent contractions. I'm smiling as I type thinking about all the women who will be yelling at the book after reading *"small, infrequent contractions."* I've never experienced these contractions and can only write the information I've gathered from reading and speaking with women. These contractions begin to move the child slowly into the proper position for birth.

Contracting muscles are something most of us can easily understand. What this looks like while birthing a business, song, church, or relationship may be harder to imagine. Allow me to continue using our story to illustrate.

As the seatbelt on the plane clicked, bringing a sense of calm, I knew I'd started a process that would lead to something new being born. I believe the conversations with Pastor Joe were contractions moving us in a different direction. Those contractions continued to push us into proper position when the church leaders joined him in asking us to serve as their next pastor. I thought that accepting the position would be the conclusion of the delivery process, but it wasn't.

It was after accepting the position that we discovered the church's financial issues. Initially, I was hurt and angry. I could not see then what is clear to me now. Labor was still occurring. If the contractions of the situation had not caused us to close the church and reopen as Legacy, it might not exist today. The contractions positioned our baby for a proper delivery.

Fear is Normal

While at first the contractions are mild and infrequent, they intensify throughout early labor. This can be a time of some anxiety. Many articles and books encourage women to distract themselves with light activity. It's not time to rush to the hospital yet, but the time is approaching quickly. The anxiety comes from knowing that their child is about to be pushed into the world with no idea how that child will be received.

As a public speaker, I understand that kind of anxiety. In my early years, my hands would shake as I walked onto the stage. I'd lay out my lengthy notes and work hard not to show my nervousness. I was about to present what was in me and I didn't know how those gathered would respond. Fear would cause me to speak quickly and fifteen pages of notes would be gone in fifteen minutes. My message may have been awesome, but my presentation didn't set it up for success.

You may be recognizing the contractions occurring in your life. Maybe you sense the previously closed doors beginning to open. You know that labor has begun and you are afraid. Afraid that what you have imagined will not become reality. Afraid that those welcoming your baby will reject it.

Those fears are normal, and they focus on elements of human behavior that are beyond your control. We all know that there are pretty and handsome people in the world, and then there are the rest of us. There are those who are extremely talented and those who are not. There are companies that do well and those that are never accepted. There are books written and published that are never purchased. There are babies born that are never loved by anyone other than their mother. It is sad, but it is true. Our job is to prepare our offspring for presentation. We cannot control the response others will have to them.

Before proceeding further, you must answer the question, *"Is the drive to deliver stronger than my fear of rejection?"*

I've spoken before congregations with all the passion I could muster while people fall asleep. People have stood up and walked out in the middle of my sermon multiple times. Some have given me the line most pastors know well -- say it with me now, *"I'm just not being fed here, so I'm being called to go somewhere else."* It always impacts me, but rejection has never stopped my delivery. I've answered the question by saying, *"My drive to deliver is greater than my fear of rejection."*

Will the regret of not delivering be worse than the pain of failing to succeed?

It doesn't matter if you're delivering a sermon, a program, a restaurant, a call center, a web interface, an app, or a song, the possibility for rejection exists. It is in these quiet moments as the positioning is completing that you must answer the question.

Will the regret of not delivering be worse than the pain of failing to succeed? What is your answer? A half-committed delivery can result in a healthy physical baby, but it will never birth a healthy destiny.

Once you move to the second stage of labor, all the energy in your body will be used to push this baby into the world. You won't have the time or inclination to think objectively. Between contractions, a few regrets may spring to mind. You may consider a few bad words. Your focus on the task at hand will prohibit you from objectively considering the cost to benefit ratio of what you are doing. So, in a sense, this is your last opportunity to pull back without damaging something. Only you and God can know the right decision in this moment.

I pray that you will have clarity. Let me share the phrase that has allowed me to push forward several times. *"Should failure occur, life doesn't end, but without a delivery it can't ever begin."*

Maybe it won't work like you think it will. Maybe success won't be achieved at the level you hope to see. While there are so many *"maybes"* that can arise when trying to assess the unknown, there is one thing that isn't a maybe, but an absolute. If you don't give birth to the baby, it will never have an opportunity to succeed.

Make up your mind. Stage two is about to begin, and I think you are ready.

CHAPTER 17

Stage 2

Have you ever watched a sporting event and noticed the extreme changes in the behavior of the athletes? Last year, I was watching a game between the Cleveland Cavilers and Oakland's Golden State Warriors. It was during the finals and it looked like the series was going to a full seven games. I watched the players make their way onto the court and greet each other with handshakes and hugs. Some of those guys had obviously known each other for a long time, some have played together; they are friends.

When the official signaled time for the jump ball, the atmosphere changed. The general on-court camaraderie ended and intense competition began. Players pushed hard to defeat their opponents. They yelled at each other and got away with as many fouls as the officials allowed. Everything changed when the game started.

The second stage of labor can often be identified by the shift in personality. As things begin to intensify, reality changes. This stage is called active labor. This means you are no longer talking in terms like *"what if"* or *"when,"* but are using the word *"now"* a lot. You are about to have a child, and suddenly the weight of the consequences and responsibility becomes a reality. The officials have signaled that the jump ball is imminent and the attitude of those delivering the destiny shifts.

The intensity of spirit changes. I'm a fairly intense person by nature, but my intensity rose to new heights during the years of building Legacy. Everything was on the line and I was hyper-aware of every detail. This intensity found a rhythm and subsided, but it remained elevated throughout the process.

While Kristy and I have always maintained reasonably strong focus, that also rose to a new level. The number of items we gave our focus to during this time was incredibly small, but we still maintained a weekly family day each Monday. We worked around the house, spent time together, and did something fun with our children. While Mondays were *"family days,"* what we talked about rarely varied. It's hard to talk freely about things you aren't focused on, and that was our issue. Our hyper-focus limited even our fun conversations.

I pray that you are healthier than we were in those days. I hope your interests expand your conversations so you can unplug on your days off. No matter where you fall on the intense focus spectrum, everything will narrow and intensify during active labor.

Watch for Moment

Clarity is your best friend as you begin the second stage of labor. In the realm of birthing a child, the processes of expectation and labor have specific time frames. It is common knowledge that a healthy gestation is nine months. A little reading will confirm that early labor will last between eight to twelve hours. There are some exceptions to these timelines, but they are universally accurate enough for most people to track their progress. We know that veering off these parameters usually signals that something is wrong. Birthing your destiny is not that simple. The timeframe of each stage manifests differently in every life.

Surf culture is big in Hawaii. Even those who don't surf know a good bit about it because of its prevalence. The goal of surfing is to position yourself in such a way that the wave you are wanting to ride rises just behind you. Letting it rise in front of you will leave you behind. Getting too far in front of the wave will cause it to simply crash over you. The surfer's goal is for their board to be picked up by the face of the wave. This is the surface of water that is actively rising out of the body of the ocean. It's at neither the top nor the bottom. When the surfer is positioned properly, the power of the rising water pushing up on the board propels the board and rider upward and forward. The combination of the surfer's weight and the angle they choose for their ride keeps the board from rising to the top of the wave and being tossed over the top.

You may have seen surfers sitting on their boards in the water for long periods of time. Often, they will sit in lines facing out to sea. Waves arrive in sets and they are waiting for the right set of waves to form. Spectators can tell when a potential set begins to approach because the line of surfers will turn toward shore. They will no longer be sitting calmly on their board, but they will have laid down on their chests and begun using both arms to paddle furiously. Two things are happening simultaneously. First, they're getting into position for that wave, and waves are not made from a template that causes them to appear in the same place, moving at the same speed. The surfer must adapt to the unique nature of each wave. Second, they are working to gain speed so when the wave rises beneath them, they can be pushed forward while maintaining control. Without intentionally gaining momentum, the wave will control them.

I've always thought that standing on a moving board in moving water was the difficult part of surfing. I was wrong. After speaking with many surfers, I've learned that proper positioning is the most difficult part to master. Because every wave is different, the timing needed to ride each one is completely unique. A skilled surfer knows when to begin paddling.

Though I'm not a surfer, I've sat in that line across the water before. The most amazing aspect was that the surfers turned and began paddling before I even saw a wave forming. They aren't looking for a wave above the water. They were looking for a depression within the water. A wave in deep water is revealed by the depression it makes. It is only when it hits the rock shelf and begins climbing that it becomes a wave above water and begins to crest.

A wave in deep water is revealed by the depression it makes.

Like the unique nature of waves, birthing your destiny is completely unique. Early labor may be completed in days, months, or even years. In some ways, I think my early labor took about five years. It was five years of revelation and situationally positioning everything within me *(mind, soul, and spirit)* to birth a church.

I can't define when early labor will transition to active labor for you, but I encourage you to watch for the depression in the water in front of you.

The leaders I work with probably get tired of hearing the phrase, *"It looks like we are going to another level."* I say that every time I see a depression in the water in front of me. It's my way of reminding myself and the team that a depression always precedes a wave. In fact, you can't experience the wave without the depression. A depression lets me know it is time to begin working to gain momentum. A wave is coming!

Active labor is when there's a notable shift in the focus of strength and energy. For nine months, the organs and muscles in the abdomen have been focused on one job. They are keeping the child safely contained inside the womb. In this stage, however, these organs and muscles turn their attention to the effort of pushing the child out into the world. The contractions will intensify, forcing the child to begin moving out of the uterus, through the cervix and into the birth canal.

We sing, *"Silent Night. Holy Night. All is calm. All is bright."* It was certainly holy, and it may have been bright, but calm and silent it was not. When Mary went into active labor and her muscles contracted, pushing the child Jesus out of her womb, the real pain of labor began. Mary didn't have an epidural. Mary wasn't quiet.

You Must Stretch

I dropped a line in chapter fifteen that I hope resonated with you. It explains the reason pain is present in the delivery process. That line was, *"The processes of conception and expectation produce a destiny bigger than your natural capacity to bring forth."* Without being too graphic, let's recognize that the baby's head is larger than the birth canal. The canal must stretch exponentially to accommodate the child. One lady described the event as pushing a bowling ball through a straw! This stretching causes pain.

I hope you are reading this book during your teenage years. I'd love to think you are living in a stable home where your needs are being met. It would be incredible if your process could be accomplished without outside distractions. In this area, the birth of a biological child has one up on the birthing a destiny. The mother is usually checked into a hospital where the staff cares for her. If she has chosen a home birth, there are usually professionals overseeing her process. Her home and potentially her other children are being cared for by friends or family so she can focus completely on bringing this child into the world. Most people reading this book are not birthing a destiny in a place without distractions. You probably have a few other things going on in your life even as you give birth.

Think about a mother giving birth while cleaning her home, watching her other children, and hosting a dinner party at the same time. Throughout most of Legacy's delivery, I was working a full-time job. This included working for a local pest control company, hanging drywall, and laboring on a construction crew. I would work eight hours in the sun then rush home to be a husband, father, and pastor. I taught three unique sermons a week until we stopped hosting Sunday night services. At the same time, I was teaching personal bible studies every evening except Monday. I was working to squeeze thirty-six hours out of twenty-four. That's what active labor looks like.

If your process has not yet involved pain, it will at this point. Progress is going to hurt. This stretching is not unique to church building. In the April episode of Chefs Table on Netflix, Chef Christina Tosi talked about giving birth to her New York based bakery, Momofuku Milk Bar. She shared how she would work all day at the Momofuku restaurant then drive to the bakery location to work into the early morning hours. She sanded and painted walls. She perfected recipes. She worked until she felt she was falling over. Yes, friends would help, but it wasn't happening without her driving the effort.

If your process has not yet involved pain, it will at this point.
Progress is going to hurt.

It is easy to see Christina today and imagine that her rise to success was painless. How hard can making pastries really be? Making one single pastry may not be difficult, but developing a destiny is. The ingredients of your destiny may be different than that of a pastry chef, but birthing it will hurt no matter what it ultimately looks like. It hurts because what you are producing is larger than your natural capacity to bring forth. This type of effort is painful. It requires everything you have to keep going. Your destiny will not emerge without it.

Restriction Comes Next

It's during active labor that you will experience another counter intuitive reality. Moving the child through the birth canal reduces its movements in every direction. The muscle contractions squeeze the child and push it into an even smaller space than the one it develops within. This is counter intuitive because most people see birthing a destiny as an expansion of life not further restrictions. It is true that expansion is coming, but not yet. Your destiny must accept further restriction before it can experience freedom.

I've mentioned the surprise when first becoming the pastor of that group of seventeen people. Standing before them, I cast a vision of expansion, painting a picture of a growing church reaching many people on the Big Island. The reality was that we were only reaching a few people, the church debt meant money was getting tighter, and my secular job at a local pest control company wasn't bringing in enough to pay my personal bills.

Every leader I know has experienced a time of great restriction before expansion came.

It would have been easier to simply quit. We were already feeling cramped in our financial and personal space, and looking into what we knew would mean even further restriction. It would have made complete sense to walk away. No one would even know about the vision inside of us. Unlike physical pregnancy, the only sign of our expectation were the words and actions coming from our lives. We could have stopped the process, but we didn't.

Every leader I know has experienced a time of great restriction before expansion came. The difference between those who birth a destiny and those who live in the destiny of others is their willingness to experience the pain and endure the restriction. The odd reality is that this labor process involves, in some ways, both giving birth and being born at the same time.

During active labor, the expectant mother is putting her focus and energy into the process, but she is still not making it happen herself. The time for intentional pushing has not arrived, but it is quickly approaching.

In active labor, your life is working hard, but there is little to be seen from the outside. You are sanding and painting a bakery that hasn't seen its first customer. You are writing and rewriting a book that no one has read. The effort is there, but the result often feels like it may never arrive. Sometimes the mixture of pain, stretching, and frustration makes it hard to breathe.

Don't Forget to Breathe

The books and articles on birthing all talk about the importance of breathing. A movie with a birth usually includes the quintessential scene of a woman whose hand is being held by a loved one. She is in pain and they are repeating the phrase, *"Just breathe."* My study has revealed that there is no single right way to breathe. The key is to simply breathe deeply and consistently.

I did not appreciate the importance of breathing until working on a construction crew. My company was hired to install the infrastructure needed to build a subdivision on the coastline in Waikoloa, Hawaii. I was hired as a laborer. My self-given title was professional hand excavation specialist. This was a nice way of saying I was paid to shovel. I shoveled rock, dirt, gravel, and anything else my bosses said needed to be shoveled. It was hard, hot work. During my first few weeks, I passed out from heat more than once. My muscles would burn so badly I'd have to stop shoveling and take a break. The saddest part was that I was a twenty-eight-year-old guy working alongside guys who were over sixty years old. I would take a break and they would never stop.

At first, I thought the problem was that most of my previous jobs were office related. I wasn't accustomed to hard labor. As my body adjusted to my environment, I did stop passing out, but my ability to shovel wasn't improving. Mr. Larry, who was in his mid-sixties, walked over to me one day and said, *"Maybe you can preach like a man, but you shovel like a girl."* I'd like to say I was offended by the sexism of his remark, but in reality, I was too frustrated by the accuracy of his meaning to take umbrage with his presentation.

Later that day, I went to him and said, *"I'm young and you are not. I should be able to do what you do. Can you teach me how you shovel?"* Now, reading this you are probably thinking, *"Shoveling is simple. Why should he need to teach you to shovel?"*

I agree that shoveling is simple, but shoveling consistently for eight hours is not. Mr. Larry agreed to teach me. He showed me how he held his hands. I wasn't that far off. Then he showed me the angle he kept his back. That made a big difference. Lastly, he showed me how to breathe. Breathing made the greatest difference. Breathing both calms and cools the body while fueling the muscles with oxygen. He said, *"If you will keep breathing, you can keep working."* It was only then that I realized that every time I shoveled, I held my breath. When I wasn't breathing I was tense, heating up, and starving my muscles for oxygen. When I learned to breathe, I began shoveling like Mr. Larry. Well, almost like him. That man was a machine, and I was blessed to work beside him.

As you move through labor, breathe. Take in the fuel your body needs to operate. In my life, I breathe when I spend time in prayer and meditation. These are moments when I talk to God, worship Him for His greatness, and listen for His direction. I have spent hours in communication with God as I prepared the foundation grade for water lines. He has blessed me with ideas as the electrical package was being molded, set, and tied. I found that the more time I spent breathing with Him, the better the birthing process went. Equally the less time I spent breathing, the more difficult things seemed to become.

There is no special way to breathe. Maybe in your life breathing means escaping to the woods to hike, hunt, fish, or working around the house. Breathing in your life may be designing and arranging table decor. One lady recently said baking is her escape. When she bakes, it refreshes her. Today Kristy and I will breathe by taking a long drive in the farm country of northwestern Ohio. Driving and talking or listening to music gives time for everything to relax. It revives me internally and energizes me to continue working.

Whatever your methodology, learning to breathe between contractions will allow you to work longer without tiring. Working while tired reduces effectiveness. Weariness will limit progress and could cause your ultimate demise. Breathe and live!

Breathing will help you keep going, but the temptation is to just stop. The thought when facing the pain and restrictions is, *"Why don't I just quit? Why keep going?"*

Why didn't we quit when faced with the pain and additional restrictions in life? Why didn't Christiana Tosi walk away from her bakery? Why didn't Jobs and Woz stop when the situation became tougher instead of easier? Why didn't Henry Ford stop when it looked like he would lose his incredible investment? Why should you keep going and refuse to pull back?

I believe that everyone who knows destiny is within them hold a common desire. It is an incredible longing to see what will be revealed if the process contained within your life is allowed to unfold.

The truth is usually simple: We didn't stop because we wanted to see what existed on the other side of the pain. It was worth it.

CHAPTER 18

Stage 3

There is no way around the pain of delivering your destiny. Before we knew that we would be pastoring a church in the Toledo metro area of Ohio, Kristy and I considered planting another church. During the conversations, we examined the process and pain we went through to plant Legacy. We were trying to figure out if the payoff was worth the price by looking again at the cost-benefit ratio. At some point Kristy said, *"The pain of building Legacy was great. The pain of leaving Legacy was worse. After considering these factors, if another Legacy Church would be the result, I'd say, 'Yes,' to the process again."*

Selfish people will not give birth to a destiny, but the strong will. You will need to be strong for the third stage of labor when the child emerges from the mother and enters the world. The intensity has been ratcheting upwards on every level, but it is in this stage that it all peaks.

By now, all the preparations that will be made have been made. There is no stopping this process. The baby is coming one way or another.

This moment differs in every life. I'm using the word *"moment,"* but the timeframe varies. The fact of the matter is that the baby can no longer fit within the safety of the womb. It must be brought into the open. In chapter 10, we looked at the unfeasibility of placing a fully developed fetus into an unprepared womb. One moment the woman is not expecting and the next moment her womb contains a fully developed fetus. At best she would be in immense, unimaginable pain and at worst she would die a terrible death. Tragically, the same is true in this stage of the birthing process of a destiny.

It's Time

At some point the baby must be born. Protected and supplied with nourishment, it will continue to grow and develop. Just as a woman who is not expecting could not survive the implantation of a fully developed fetus, no human can internally carry another fully developed human.

Because Kristy was a physically small woman and our first son was physically large, she had to have labor induced. During pregnancy, Kristy developed gestational diabetes which exacerbated his growth. As some point, the doctors knew that a natural birth was not going to be possible if delivery didn't progress quickly. The child was simply going to become too big to carry.

Today, both of our sons are physically bigger than their mother. Holding back delivery would have eventually ripped her apart and ended any possibility of her producing again. Failure to deliver the child would have eventually destroyed her.

I wonder how many people have held onto their dreams too long. There is no way to know the answer, but in a few conversations over the years, I've walked away thinking I may have seen a glimpse of this reality. As they began to tell me about their life, there were quick flashes of a life they had been planning for, but never lived. You may hear it if you listen closely.

Sometimes it's revealed in stories from a young person who speaks as though they were older. Those who have lived a long time will usually speak about the past more than the future. They have lived a good life and experienced things worth talking about.

When the young person speaks about the past more than the future, it could reveal a destiny that was never delivered.

While this is a difficult thing to see, it's far worse when experienced, but it doesn't have to be your future! If you are living in the shell of what might have been, I pray God's grace over your life. You must also understand that your life isn't over. Don't die before you are dead! Shift your focus forward and walk away from the destructive power of undelivered destiny. You will begin by conceiving again. As long as you're alive, greatness can be birthed from your life!

After physical labor, what you are birthing moves from being protected, fed, and covered by you and your team alone. It is in no way ready to live on its own, but this process provides it a measure of separation from you.

Your destiny is not fully birthed until it could be taken by another and developed into its full potential.

Separation from the mother too soon almost ensures the child will not survive. In a healthy pregnancy, however, once labor has occurred, the child could be raised by someone else entirely. Adopted children are taken from their birth mothers after labor and entrusted to strangers. Those strangers did not conceive them, expect them, or push them from their womb, but they are able to raise them into maturity. Your destiny is not fully birthed until it could be taken by another and developed into its full potential.

Your book is birthed when its idea has moved from your mind onto a page, through the editing process, and could be published and read by others. A song is birthed when it could be taken by another artist and recorded in the studio. A business has been birthed when another CEO could sit in your chair. A church is birthed when another leader could take over and keep it strong and prosperous. It doesn't mean your child can live independent of anyone, but it does mean a level of personal sustainability has been achieved.

Through physical labor, you present your product to the world and sustainability develops. In some ways, this is the most beautiful of moments. You know that you are about to live the dream of holding this child, and the process is in motion. The only thing left to do is finally push your child out into the world. You have been preparing a long time for this moment.

When You Tear

The third stage is when the stretching of labor is at its greatest. There's no other way for the child to pass from your body and into the world. Stretching hurts. It extends you beyond your normal limitations. It pulls at you until you feel as if you are being ripped apart. You are stretched as you deal with people you wouldn't normally be friends with, situations you have never faced before, and you feel the weight of responsibility on your shoulders.

The tissues of the body can only stretch so far before they tear. I wish this were only true when speaking of birthing a child, but tearing is likely in every kind of labor. This is a dangerous time in the birthing of a destiny. When you are stretched to the point of tearing, it creates a wound that must heal, and as with any open wound, the risk of infection is great.

I know what it is like to be torn.

The humorous reality is that I was most confident just before I was stretched the most. The church was growing, and while we had experienced a tough start, things seemed to be aligning. I was feeling good about where we were in our process. I knew we had a long way to go, but in two years, the church had gone from seventeen people to over one hundred and thirty. We were financially strong for our size, and it looked like the baby was going to have an easy birth. I had no idea that I was entering some of the hardest years of my life.

Three events occurred that stretched me too far.

The first happened when I reached out to other pastors. Island living was great, but I was a thousand miles from friends in the middle of the Pacific. We were navigating waters I had never been in before, and I didn't know where to turn. So I reached out to an older pastor in the area. I knew he was from a different Christian tradition than my own, but as the pastor represented the local Christian pastor's social group, I didn't think that would matter.

From the beginning of the conversation, I was excited. I shared my story with him. I was open about our successes and our failures. We talked about the importance of building a good relationship, especially in a small town on an island. He was very kind on the phone, but a few days later I began to hear from church members that he was speaking poorly about me around town. Soon I discovered that he was using information I'd shared with him negatively. It seemed like he was actively trying to hurt me. I couldn't believe what was happening.

I was devastated. We were just beginning to see what this baby would look like, and someone was already trying to destroy us. When this pastor used my efforts to connect as an opportunity to hurt me, something tore within me.

I went into a time of deep depression. To the great people of our congregation, I remained positive and encouraging. Externally, I revealed little of my true feelings, but internally I was devastated. Cynicism began flooding my internal feelings and thoughts. It became difficult to talk about what was going on because the dominant reality of my life was not something I could share. I was surrounded by people and feeling alone.

On the heels of this experience came the second event. A family we loved, worked closely with, and trusted greatly announced they were leaving us. Not only that, but they were launching their own church. While I understood their desires and reasons, it didn't lessen the pain of their departure. I confess that the tears were many and the pain was deep.

The third event impacted us and the rest of the world. We moved to the Big Island in 2005. 2006 revealed the mortgage crisis, and by the time 2008 arrived, the economic recession was in full swing. Legacy was just under three years old. You would think that a church that old would classify as being born, but that thought would be incorrect. We lacked clarity on who God was calling us to be, both as a church and as a leadership team. Financially, we were living month to month. This was the time when pushing really began.

During the recession, tourism to the islands slowed down and construction almost stopped altogether. The people of the church were faithful, but jobs were quickly disappearing. Many were forced to move their families in search of work. A good number of those remaining had made a good living in construction and tourism but were now collecting unemployment. Legacy was hit hard. I was afraid and feeling helpless. The tear in my life grew.

The recession coincided with that family launching a church and several other families leaving with them. One Sunday morning, before service, our reality was made crystal clear. The atmosphere was usually loud and full of laughter, but this day was quiet. The few who had arrived early for service were sitting silently or talking in small groups. Kristy and I were standing in front of the stage, just before service began, when a woman approached. She looked up at us and said with a wry grin, *"Where is everybody? They are dropping like flies around here."* In that instant, I felt like ten thousand pounds had been dropped on my head. I didn't know if we had what it took to go forward, but I knew we had gone too far to turn around.

The baby wasn't yet delivered, the pain was growing, and we were too far along to stop the process. This church had to be born! There was no going back!

I want to be clear, I'm not crying today. Some readers will be people who were with us as we walked that road. Some of those I've referenced in these three stories may do me the honor of perusing these pages. I have no regrets, animosities, or frustrations over these past events. I am not crying today. Those who made decisions or statements that caused pain are not the focus. I was in a birthing process. I was bringing a destiny from within me. In these pages, I'm doing my best to paint a real picture of what it means to birth a destiny from your life.

It tore me, but your experience can be different. No, you can't eliminate the pain, but you can direct the process. Doctors will sometimes intentionally cut the tissue at the points of greatest strain to eliminate tearing. While on the surface it seems to result in the same outcome, the effects are different. Surgical incisions are always better than having your flesh torn. The lines are cleaner, tension is intentionally released, and repairs are made with minimizing scarring.

Emotion and Spiritual Realities

This is a driving factor behind the writing of this book. So much has been written on building or creating almost anything. Church building strategies are plentiful today. Material on building businesses fills bookshelves in stores. You can find plenty of instructions on how to write songs, books, or articles. Help on intentionally and strategically moving through the processes emotionally and spiritually, however, is not as easy to find.

In the process of physical labor, you are on your own.

During this stage, clarity is vital. You may be blessed to have people cheering you on. I pray that you do. Do not mistake their cheering for understanding. In the process of physical labor, you are on your own. The child often resists being born because the world is scary. Those around you may have an idea of what you are birthing, but they cannot have the deep connection to it that you do.

Don't judge them harshly when they lose focus on your birthing. I've witnessed the frustration of others as they realize that the all-encompassing activity of their life is a passing interest to others. In a worst-case scenario, what you are birthing is seen as a threat to some. These realities manifest in different ways. A mild form of disinterest may be revealed by family or friends asking, *"Do you have to talk about that stuff all the time?"* A more severe manifestation could be someone actively working to abort the baby during birth.

While I was writing this, the iconic restaurant chain IHOP announced a name change to IHOb to market their new line of burgers. No doubt they had been planning this move for a long time. They had not only released media, but they had changed physical signage and social media handles as well. Some articles speculated that the name change was permanent, but others recognized that this established company was still trading publicly under their original name. The shift only lasted a few weeks, but it was their process of birthing a new identity as a burger restaurant. However, not everyone was happy about them bringing their new identity into the world.

Wendy's, the well-known burger chain, saw the birth of IHOb as a potential threat to their profits. Wendy's responded to IHOb's announcement by Tweeting, *"Remember when you were like 7 and thought changing your name to Thunder BearSword would be super cool? Like that, but our cheeseburgers are still better."* [39]

One Twitter user asked if Wendy's was going to just lay down and let IHOb sell burgers on their block. Wendy's responded, *"Not really afraid of the burgers from a place that decided pancakes were too hard."* [40]

I never thought that the IHOb name would stick – they were just working to give birth to a new reputation that would make their brand attractive to a larger number of potential customers. Wendy's saw their labor as a direct threat and was pushing back.

In your life, some will recognize the value of what you are birthing. They will celebrate with you. Others will be marginally interested, but their interest will fade. The most difficult group will be those who see your destiny as a threat to their current existence. Recognizing these realities will allow you to deal with them.

In hindsight, I could have anticipated the family leaving us and launching their own church. I could have identified the impact it would have on our organization and planned accordingly. I should have known that the pastor of the established church would see the launch of Legacy as a potential threat to his organization. Threatening him was the last thing on my heart or mind, but birthing something new is always a threat to anything that's already in the environment.

If I had properly anticipated these realities, I could have made intentional incisions in my life and limited the damage that resulted from tearing. We could have stopped the internal bleeding and made certain the pieces fit back together. I survived and eventually thrived, but I could have been healthier. I'm praying these stories will help you remain healthy during the labor process.

Practical Steps

Information without application does little to ease the situation. So, here are a few practical steps you can take to intentionally ease the strain stretching produces.

1. Identify your pain points.

In my life, it's always been relationships. It's not that I've had terrible relationships – I'm just sensitive to changes in them. You may handle changing relationships easily, but you do have pain points. Identifying your areas of sensitivity will allow you to pay close attention to those areas of your life and be intentional about releasing the building pressure.

Be proactive in dealing with the pain points you identify. Don't wait for the event to occur before you respond. Anticipating realities allows you to prepare yourself for the shift and minimize the hurt. You may still feel pain, but it will be managed pain. Managed pain is easier to live with.

2. Become brutally honest with yourself.

Lying to yourself never helps you move forward. The fact is that most people don't care about you or your destiny. Fewer still will invest heavily in helping deliver your destiny. Recognizing that most people will only give their attention if they will receive something in return allows you to operate on a realistic plane. Becoming brutally honest about the realities allows you to develop proper expectations and releases tension.

3. Refuse to hold grudges.

There wasn't a bad person in any of the stories I shared. The pastor of the established church could have handled the situation better, but he wasn't inherently evil. In some ways he was afraid. It would be ridiculous for me to hold a grudge against him for trying to act in his organization's best interest. Most people aren't evil. They just don't share your concerns or interests. In truth, you probably don't care about their interests either. I certainly wasn't trying to hurt his organization, but I wasn't building it either. That doesn't make anyone evil. It does make us all human.

4. Don't hold off too long.

I'm not suggesting you begin making cuts quickly. You will never relieve all the pressure from stretching. I am suggesting that a cut is better than a tear and it won't help you to wait too long. A friend that is stretching you beyond your limits should be cut. This can be a conversation where you let them know you will be off their grid for a time or one that severs the relationship altogether. You must decide what it should look like, but making the cut before tearing begins will be healthier in the long run.

5. Trust the process.

You know what is within you. While you're stretching and under pressure, it is easy to back off and second guess why you are giving birth at all. In reality, what you knew to be necessary before the process began is still necessary in the middle of it. Don't let your current situation steal your previous revelation.

6. Push.

The bottom line in physical delivery is that you must push. You must push to deliver through the pain. Push through the distraction. Push through the hurt caused by others. Push through the mistakes you will make along the way. There will be many things that will begin and end, but one thing that must be ever-present in your time of physical delivery is that you must push. Don't stop pushing your destiny forward.

Pushing is not one consistent effort. It is a rhythmic process of contracting and releasing muscles. In the next chapter, we will talk about the rhythm of delivery.

That beautiful moment when the Christ Child was transitioning into the world, stretching and pain were present. There is no doubt that Mary was a strong woman, but even the strongest people cry out when the pain is great. The moment physical labor began, Mary's pain increased and no doubt her voice was heard.

No matter what your destiny may be, you will experience a period like this. Your stories will be different, but the pain will be the same. The stretching will be the same.

In this moment of your life, a mentor or coach will be invaluable. Your body is tired, and your emotions are frayed. You are at your most vulnerable, and you are not fully capable of caring for yourself. You need someone to help you progress, to help you remain focused and encourage you. You need someone to correct you when your natural reflex to pain causes you to begin moving in a wrong direction.

Doubts and fears plague those in active labor. Women throughout history have cried out, *"I don't think I can do this!"* The reality is that she is doing exactly what God has designed her to do. It is painful and sometimes scary, but don't forget that it is also within the parameters of the God-designed capabilities of life!

Find someone that is willing to be your Joseph. Develop that mentor or coach who can tell you, **"You can do this!"**

It's good for someone to be there in that moment and remind you of this reality. Mary had Joseph. Who is your Joseph? We often forget the role of this great man in the birth of Jesus. We don't have a lot of specific information on everything he did. We do know a few things. First, he was willing to support Mary as she worked through something he could not fully understand. Second, he was thoughtful enough to keep her as comfortable as their situation would allow. Third, Joseph was present as Mary went through the process of delivering her destiny into the world.

She was designed for this role, and Joseph was there to remind her of that reality whenever she doubted it. God designed you. He placed within you the potential for birthing a destiny. He created you with all the potential, as well as the ability to survive the delivery! You can make it! Find someone that is willing to be your Joseph. Develop that mentor or coach who can tell you, *"You can do this!"*

It's interesting to note that while the active delivery part of the process is the most feared, it is also the shortest. The time-frames on conception and expectation are usually measured in months. Delivery, hours. No matter how long it seems like it is taking, this part of the process will pass, and there is great joy on the other side!

I wrote earlier that what you have given birth to could be taken by another and thrive, but the beauty is that you don't have to be separated. You can enjoy the blessing of what you have produced for many years to come!

CHAPTER 19

Learn to Pause

The emotional pendulum swings wildly during delivery. Laughing can quickly become crying. Anticipation can morph to fear. Sometimes it seems like it's taking forever for this baby to leave your womb, but in comparison to the other stages of delivering your destiny, the delivery is short. Your emotions cannot be the gauge by which you measure progress.

Just as the monitors track the progress of the baby, advisors and mentors help you track the progress of your destiny. Patience is a virtue, but not a natural one for many of us. It is usually forced waiting that teaches patience. Birthing something doesn't happen swiftly. It is a process that occurs in waves. Intense and focused action relents to rest. In certain moments you must push hard. In others you should relax.

Finding moments for relaxation is critical. When labor was induced, things got a bit crazy in the room. Talon was not progressing out of the birth canal and his heart rate was dropping. At one point, a doctor was pulling from below while a nurse was laying on top pushing from above. It was wild. Even during that crazy time, moments were found for Kristy to relax. One nurse had the job of watching the machine monitoring Kristy's contractions.

She would periodically call out, *"Hold,"* and everything would stop. They would encourage Kristy to rest and relax for a moment.

Soon, the monitor would indicate the start of the next contraction. The nurse would say, *"Ready. Now."* The doctor would then direct the team by saying, *"Push!"* Kristy would push, the doctor would pull, and the nurse would begin shoving down on Kristy's belly again.

Eventually, Talon was born.

Without relaxation, you will exhaust yourself. We have already made it clear that without completing delivery, both the baby and the mother would die. Scripture teaches that thieves arrive in a location to kill, steal, and destroy. The same verse lets us know that Jesus came to earth so that we could have an abundant life![41]

The destiny within you is meant not to destroy you but elevate your life. You can have this baby!

The Role of Mentors

Learning the rhythm of delivery is not easy, but a mentor or coach can provide the same services as the doctors and nurses did in the delivery room. Only you can decide whether you listen to their instructions. Their advice will save you from wasting effort and could keep you from unintentionally harming your baby.

An epidural is a wonderful medical invention. Medication is applied to the spinal column and the pain of active childbirth is blocked, allowing the mother becomes much more comfortable. The downside is that she is less aware of the natural rhythms of her body. This means she can be pushing when her body is trying to relax. One doctor I spoke to said pushing at the wrong time is one reason some children are born with broken bones. The mother's body is both pushing and holding, squeezing the baby. While is not uncommon that a baby suffers an injury while traveling through the birth canal, it is more common among those who push when they should be relaxed.

The point is that the pain of labor will limit your objectivity. Listening to advisors is one way to ensure you are operating at maximum efficiency.

We were blessed with a pastor who understood rhythm. I was pushing in every way I knew and was exhausted. One day, I shared my daily schedule with my pastor. I was shocked when he didn't congratulate me for all the hard work I was doing. Instead he began telling me where I needed to pull back. The issue was that he was telling me to pull back on things that I knew were good things to be doing.

Listening to his advice seemed counterintuitive, but I listened anyway. I'm glad I did. Learning the rhythm of delivery caused me to push at the right times. At first, I was frustrated by what seemed like a delay in completing the goal. In time, however, I recognized that pushing became more productive when they were punctuated by pauses.

If this book were written without punctuation marks it would be difficult to read it effectively because the periods commas quotation marks question marks and every other form of punctuation are indicators of pauses which create order and allow for the text to be read most effectively. That amazing run-on sentence was not easy to read. You probably inserted your own punctuation, pausing in the appropriate places. If you read the sentence aloud as written, you are probably out of breath. That's delivery without pauses.

Life without Pauses

Many things motivate people to live without pauses. Pride can cause you to think you don't need to pause. Fear can convince you that you can't afford to pause. Impatience can cause you to race past a pause. All of these can cause you to become tired, weak, and ineffective. When pauses are inserted, you can move more effectively through the process.

The pauses allow you to gather strength and push. It provides time for your body to stretch, adjusting to the new reality. Maybe most importantly, a pause allows an opportunity to gain not only perspective on progress but also time to align your efforts. Effectiveness is key in this stage of delivery. Conserving energy and guarding against wasted efforts is important. Your objectivity is compromised, and your emotions are strained. The pause gives you a moment to recalibrate both and receive guidance from those around you.

Your ability to pause and adjust will directly impact how your destiny emerges from the womb. This stage will reveal the scope and size of what God has placed within you. Your job is to be as accommodating as possible. Stretch as far as you are able. Become intentional about making incisions before tearing. Delivery is hard and painful.

The pause gives you a moment to recalibrate both and receive guidance from those around you.

In a physical delivery, once the process has begun, it must be completed. In the delivery of a destiny, you can choose to stop at any time in but a moment. A business destiny can be walked away from. A relational destiny can be refused with a word. The only thing that will birth your destiny is your determination to see it through. This means that what you are giving birth to will be no bigger than your narrowest restriction.

It's Up to You

Some people wonder why their business, ministry, or relationship has stopped growing. The answer is, *"That's how far you stretched."*

There was an entrepreneur who launched a fresh bread company and hated to get up early. He made great bread, but it was never ready for sale before three o'clock in the afternoon. No matter how much wonderful bread he baked, he sold very little because, by that time, most of the households had already purchased their bread for the day. People pleaded with him to change his sleeping habits, but he refused. He was convinced that customers would change their habits to accommodate his schedule once they knew how good his bread was. Alas, most people never tried his bread. His business went under because he refused to stretch. He couldn't pay the price of changing his sleeping habits.

Everyone has limitations. At some point, everyone finds their stretch limit. That point determines the size and scope of their destiny.

In his book, *"Leadership Pain: The Classroom for Growth,"* author Samuel Chand writes, *"When you interpret your pain as bigger--more important, more threatening, more comprehensive--than your vision, you'll redefine your vision down to the threshold of your pain."*[42] He says it brilliantly. Using childbirth, I'll say it this way. Your ability to stretch determines the size of your baby.

No one likes the process. I don't know anyone who enjoyed what physical birth was doing to them, but you can't deliver the destiny without the pain. Thankfully the pain doesn't last forever.

The Future is Coming

I don't remember exactly how long the experiences shared in chapter eighteen affected my daily life. I do know that they took time to heal. Eventually, that pastor and I developed a cordial relationship. He even invited me to join the ministerial group he helped lead. We remained friends with the family that left us to launch their own church, and we're still friends with them today. The phrase, *"They are dropping like flies around here,"* became well known around Legacy. After the church grew strong, we would reference that phrase when telling the story of our journey.

The pain was real and impacting. It changed me forever, but the pain itself eventually faded into a strong connection to the future.

I'll never forget the moment I first saw the faces of my boys. They were not fully born, but their heads were visible. Both times my thought was similar. That child is going to live beyond me. He will begin where I end. I meant that in every sense. I pray that our children will stand upon the platform of our lives and reach beyond the level we attained. Kristy and my marriage has been great, and I pray their marriages are better. I've been fairly successful in my calling and work, and I pray they are far more successful. In short, I hope that every area of their lives is positioned for success because they are my children. They are my connection to a future I won't see.

Mary and Joseph exited the Earth many years ago, but we tell their story because of who was born from Mary's womb. What you birth connects you to the future! You want that future to be bright.

Some people decide that having children is not the right choice for their lives. This is true of both individuals and couples. To our knowledge, Paul the apostle was never married or had children. That did not stop him from birthing something from his life that connected him with the future.

Paul authored much of the New Testament. He was also a church planter who started many of the churches we read about in the bible – and a mentor to many young men who were moving into areas of ministry. Birthing writings, churches, and spiritual development in youth connected him to the future.

Your Destiny is Here

As your destiny enters the world, it is as if a tethered arrow has been shot. It is flying faster than you can travel. It is going beyond your life. It is attaching to a future you may never see but are connected to. That is why the price of delivery is worth paying!

Every contraction of your life is moving you closer to delivering your destiny! That business, career, relationship, family, book, recording deal, or whatever you are birthing is becoming a reality. It is leaving the womb and entering your arms. It is slimy, wet, helpless, and hungry, but it is in your arms. You are no longer birthing a destiny. Your destiny is here!

On July 14, 1999, the nurse looked at me with a smile. She was holding Talon in her arms. He was wrapped tightly in a blue blanket. She took a step toward me and offered me the child. I'd held many children before, but this time was different. This was my son.

I took Talon and stared into his face. I was astonished to realize that his head looked wrong. It was a perfect cone shape. He could have been a cast member for the 1993 science fiction movie Coneheads without any prosthetics! I didn't know what to think. Turning to the nurse, I asked if he was okay, and she quickly assured me that everything was fine. Some children experience this at birth, but their heads adjust quickly. That was the case with Talon.

My point is that upon delivery of your destiny, you may face sudden surprises. Be ready. A lot can change during delivery. What you see as your future emerges may not be exactly what you are expecting. Don't worry. Don't throw it away too quickly. Don't discount the beauty and wonder that you are holding in your arms.

I held Talon and felt a father's pride, burden, and joy all at the same time...for the first time. Tears welled up in my eyes as I whispered to him, *"Hello son. I have some things to tell you. 'The Lord your God is One Lord'.*[43] *He loves you and I love you."* These were the first words I said to both of my children.

At the time of this writing, we are looking forward to Talon's nineteenth birthday. Tyrian is now sixteen. Kristy and I have spent the last nineteen years raising young men. Today, they shave, drive, work, date, and their conversations consist of talking about life beyond school. I can see glimmers of the men they will become. Either of them could survive on their own today if they had to, but when they were born, they were dependent. Yes, they were separate and totally dependent. What Kristy and I had dreamed about for many months was now being held in our arms. It was perfect.

As the last contractions fade in your life, enjoy the moment. Hold that business card in your hand and smile. Strum the chords to that song on the guitar one more time just to enjoy it yourself. Look through the chapters of your book for a moment recognizing what you have brought forth. Enjoy the moment of delivery.

You are tired and maybe in an unfamiliar environment. You are now accompanied by something you have carried, but not really met before. It is a quiet time, a precious time. If you are not careful, you will begin to move too quickly. Take the time to let things settle. It's ok to take a moment. Don't worry. The moment won't be too long.

In just a few minutes, that beautiful baby will begin to cry. It will be hungry, and it will be your job to feed it. That cry will begin a cycle that will not end until your destiny can stand on its own. That cry will symbolize that delivery is over and the next and final stage has begun.

It's time to raise your baby.

PART 4

Realization

CHAPTER 20

The Realization

Jillian was born six pounds three ounces. Her parents, Randy and Sue, were excited. They had gone through the process and their daughter was healthy. Everything had gone well, and thirty hours after giving birth, Sue was given the word that she and Jillian could go home.

Randy pulled the car up as the nurse wheeled out Sue and Jillian. After placing their newborn into her car seat, the family drove home and placed Jillian into a cute bassinet. In moments, she was asleep. The house was quiet. They were home.

Suddenly, an unusual emotion gripped Sue as waves of panic mixed with joy washed over her. She thought, *"I really have a baby."*

That feeling is not limited to parenting a child. It is the natural feeling after working toward a goal and finally finding yourself holding the object of your obsession. It can be a disconcerting recognition. What you dreamed could become, has become, and is now in your hands.

I've called this section of the book *"The Realization."* The word realization means to become fully aware of something, to cause something to happen, and to give physical form to something. Through this process, your actions have caused conception to occur. Conception became expectation. What was conceived was given the time and space to develop a physical form. The birthing process brought your destiny to the world. It is only then that you can become fully aware of what you have given birth to.

The focus of your dreams has become the focus of your reality. This is when you hold your dream in your hands for the first time. The realization stage of delivering your destiny introduces what you have been working on to the world. It's a time of excitement, beauty, wonder, and amazement. You have worked hard to get here. Your diligence and patience have resulted in realizing the beginnings of your destiny. Enjoy the moment and know that the business, book, career, or whatever you are looking at, still needs your help to achieve its full potential.

The focus of your dreams has become the focus of your reality.

From the last push and first cry, Mary recognized the unique nature of what she held in her arms. This baby looked like any other baby, but she knew that there was something special. The angel Gabriel had been clear about who and what this boy would be before conception even occurred. There was no way for Mary and Joseph to know how everything would work out, but they knew the future was going to be unique. The potential held within this child was unlike anything they had ever known. I suggest that the potential you hold is equally as unique.

No, you have not birthed the Son of God. You have, however, brought forth something completely unusual in every way. It may look like others of its kind, but there are subtle differences that will become clear over time.

I remember standing center stage in Kona looking out into the assembled crowd. They had arrived at Legacy to worship Jesus. Some of them had been part of the church for a while, but there were many new faces as well. The economy was still hurting, and many had left, but things were looking up. Surveying the room, I realized that almost all the chairs in the auditorium were filled.

I'd not seen this for a long time. The excitement was incredible. The wave of emotion was overwhelming. The thought that came to my mind was, *"This is really going to work. We survived the crash and we are growing. We have a baby!"*

In this moment, the word *"potential"* summarizes your life and situation. In your heart and mind, the door to the future swings open once you realize that your baby has survived its birth. The world has yet to feel its impact, but you recognize its capacity. Your baby's potential hasn't been tapped, but it exists. You are ready for the world to recognize what you have given birth to.

Your Interaction

Just like every other stage, the realization demands a shift in how you interact with your baby. Until now, it was part of you. While you are still inextricably connected, it now has some separation. Your interaction must shift for healthy development into maturity to begin.

Jim launched his landscaping company by himself. He personally sold his services then maintained the yards. Over time the accounts grew, but Jim refused to hire anyone. As the owner and founder, he believed that no one cared more about his business or customers than he did. His service was fantastic, but it was also unsustainable. He soon maxed out the number of customers he could consistently serve. He became tired from working all the time and frustrated because this life wasn't what he imagined it to be when he launched the company.

Jim would not allow the company to develop its own identity, to grow past him. Ultimately, it dominated his life and world. Before the company, Jim would dream of the vacations he would take and the life he would enjoy. These things never happened. The customers were there. He had the knowledge and skills needed, but Jim couldn't make the transition from delivery to realization. Jim never allowed his baby to live outside of him.

Jim's destiny had incredible potential, but he would not allow it to be realized. He would not shift how he thought about and interacted with his baby. Eventually, the cost of being a business owner became too much. Jim pulled back on the number of customers he had and began looking for a job at another landscaping company. His destiny as a business owner was cut short.

Jim isn't alone. There are songwriters who dream of a career writing music but refuse to allow others to hear them. There are books written by authors who will not publish it. There are business ideas that remain trapped inside of the visionary. Don't trap your baby! Transition your relationship and allow your destiny to grow.

Practical Steps

There are a few practical steps you can take toward realization. Let me give you a few of them.

1. Name your baby.

Historically, families were not able to identify the gender of a child until birth. No doubt, couples discussed options based on family traditions, but they didn't assign a name until after birth. A name is important because it tells the world how to identify your offspring. It differentiates your child all the others. Until now, terms like, *"your baby"* were enough of an indicator, but that was when the child was unrealized. Once the child is born, it needs a name!

My parents did not decide on a name for my brother for several days after he was born. He had the surname Sutton, but not a name that would differentiate him from all other Suttons. It's possible that you could give birth to something without a need for a name, but if you don't know what to call your offspring, no one else will either.

One morning, my mother was reading the paper and saw a headline concerning the baseball player Andre Dawson. She knew nothing about baseball, but she did like the name. Later that day, our father and mother announced to Regan and me that our brother's name was Dawson. Naming your child is the first step to what you've birthed being able to stand alone.

There aren't too many nameless people roaming around today, but there are many nameless destinies.

You may be reading these paragraphs thinking that I'm addressing something obvious. I agree that there aren't too many nameless people roaming around today, but there are many nameless destinies. I believe many people are identifying themselves with past positions rather than future destinies.

When my sons were born, I was still Micah, but I also became Talon and Tyrian's father. My sons connect me to a future I will not see. They needed to be named. The birth of your destiny doesn't change who you are, but it changes how you are connected to the future. A name provides an identity.

George was a young man with great potential. He had been raised in a pastor's home and knew that he would become a pastor. During his years of training and education, he worked many different jobs. The day came when George was asked to serve as the senior pastor of a small church. He accepted and began doing the work of ministry in that community.

Because the church was small, George continued to work in the secular world. At this time, he was an account manager for a variable data printing company. George dreamed of the day he would be serving in ministry full-time. Ministry was in his heart. When George was asked about his occupation publicly, he never said he was a pastor. He would always answer, *"I'm an account manager for a variable data printing company."*

When asked why he did that, George responded, *"I just feel uncomfortable telling people I'm a pastor. It's just awkward to me."* The reality is that while George was called to the pastoral role, dreamed of expanding that role in his life, and was doing the job as a pastor, he had not named the baby. He wasn't giving others a name by which to call his destiny. Eventually, George named the baby and is still serving in a pastoral capacity many years later.

Name your baby!

2. Introduce your baby to others.

Talk about where you are going! The more you talk about your destiny, the more solidified it becomes in your heart and mind. There is great power in stating something out loud. It changes your dynamic with the subject matter.

Educators around the world laud the value of reading aloud. It connects the reader to the material through their eyes and their ears. The reinforcement increases both understanding and recollection. The same occurs when dealing with your destiny. The more you talk about it the more comfortable you become negotiating your new reality. It is a game changer.

Introduce your destiny to people who can relate to your journey.

Talking about your destiny is powerful and who you discuss it with is important. There are some people who are driven to find fault and issue with everything. During this time, when your destiny is young, words of wisdom are invaluable, but words of negativity are destructive.

Introduce your destiny to people who can relate to your journey. I applaud writers who join authors' groups and entrepreneurs who join business groups. They are surrounding themselves with others who recognize where they are and what they are doing. People like these can add value by making suggestions and be encouraging. Introduce your baby to the right people.

The Big Entrance

Your destiny's entrance to the world is an important moment. Your offspring will play a major role in how you are viewed by those around you and by future generations. Children are a reflection of their parents.

When you read the name Steve Jobs, what did you think about next? What does the name Bill Gates bring to mind? How about the names Thomas Edison, Rosa Parks, George Washington, Martin Luther King Jr, Hedy Lamarr, or George Washington Carver? More than likely, those names instantly brought to mind the companies, inventions, revolutions, or nations birthed by these men and women. Their destiny became the lenses through which they are viewed.

Mary showed an incredible understanding of this nuance. While she was still expecting, she went to visit her cousin Elizabeth. Scripture records part of their conversation. During their greetings, Mary said something interesting. She said: *"Oh, how my soul praises the Lord. How my spirit rejoices in God my Savior! For he took notice of his lowly servant girl, and from now on all generations will call me blessed."* [44]

God has never seeded a destiny for which you need be embarrassed

---

Mary understood that generations to come would look back on her life and call her blessed. Their judgement would not be based on who she married, the specific job she worked, or where she lived. Mary understood that future generations would judge her based on her baby.

What you give birth to will represent you. This is why we dress babies up in the latest fashions, spending lots of time and money to present their child well. The baby doesn't care if it was introduced naked, but the parents know they will be judged by their offspring. When I see a child acting badly, I never think the child is bad, but often think, *"Where are the parents?"* Children are a reflection of their parents.

You will be judged by the destiny you birth. Don't rush things. Let it develop properly. Throughout this book, I've said I was addressing those who believe God has placed something unique within them. God has never seeded a destiny for which you need be embarrassed. A God-designed destiny will always be one for which you can be proud. Your job is to care for it properly and raise it well.

Your destiny is not yet ready to be released, but you are well on your way!

CHAPTER 21

Identifying the Gaps

The enemy of realization is imagination. Imagination cannot change reality, but it does set our expectations. The images and situations created by your imagination before your child is born cannot accurately portray reality. Few realities supersede the creations of the imagination.

I shared with you that when Talon was placed in my arms by the nurse, I looked down into his face and saw his cone-shaped head. It freaked me out! One would think that she would have prepared me for this moment, but no one said a thing! My shock and concern were so intense that I immediately blocked Kristy's view of our son. She was saying, *"Let me see him,"* but I did not turn around until I received clarity from the nurse that everything was ok.

I immediately loved my son, but nothing in my imagination had visualized this reality. That was the problem I faced. In my mind, Talon was born with a normal head, but reality revealed otherwise. It took a few minutes and an explanation from the nurse to help me reconcile the two. Birthing a destiny has similarities to my experience with Talon's birth.

The strong internal vision propels you forward. It causes you to make the sacrifices, handle the uncertainties, and push through the pain. Your imagination paints a wonderful picture. How many destinies would have survived if imagination revealed things accurately? Would you be quick to agree to conception if every battle to be fought and every pain to be endured was part of your preliminary dreams? It's my thought that fewer babies would be conceived.

The imagination is a powerful tool created by God and given to humanity. It has the power to bless and to hurt.

We know that in the conversation Gabriel had with Mary, he said she had found favor with God. He said she was blessed. The angel said she would have a child whose father was God. Gabriel said her son would be the Savior of God's people. No doubt Mary began imagining the reality that she would experience. The only example she could have used was her knowledge of kings of the Earth. I can't tell you exactly what Mary imagined, but I doubt that traveling far from home during her later stages of expectation was part of her picture. Mary's imagination probably didn't paint a portrait of her giving birth in a stable surrounded by barn animals accompanied only by her husband. Her concept of what it meant to birth the Son of God probably didn't include the rejection he would face or the many attempts to trap and destroy Him. She certainly didn't and couldn't imagine watching Jesus die on a cross that He didn't deserve.

Everything the angel foretold occurred. Nothing Gabriel said was wrong, misleading, or inaccurate. It simply didn't explain in detail how each part of this prophecy would come to pass. There was no way that Mary had a clear understanding of every part of her process, and neither will you.

The imagination is a powerful tool created by God and given to humanity. It has the power to bless and to hurt. The discrepancy between imagined outcomes and reality can drive someone to depression or even total despair. I'm calling these discrepancies "*gaps.*" The gap is where the imagined experience differs from the reality. These gaps become primary obstacles realizing your destiny.

Common Obstacles

While every individual experience is different, there are a few common obstacles everyone birthing a destiny will navigate when realization begins. By understanding reality a little better, we can adjust our imagination and move with confidence into a God-designed destiny. The key is managing the gap between what we imagine and what we realize. In the remainder of this chapter, I'll describe three common gaps, and in chapter twenty-two, we will look at possible ways to manage the gaps.

The Expression Gap

The first obstacle is the expression gap. This is how your off-spring is expressed in the world. It encompasses the appearance, natural tendencies, and gifts of your baby. I know the tendency is to say, *"None of those things matter! I will love them anyway!"* You will love them anyway, but these things do matter. They matter a lot!

> *No one imagines an insignificant company, a horrible song sounding, or an unread book.*

The retail industry spends huge amounts of resources determining how something will be expressed. Experts are consulted on how every product should look and feel. Fashion designers make millions of dollars to develop the clothes that people around the world wear to express themselves. These are all objects designed to appeal to the consumer. Companies know that if you like the way something is expressed, you are more likely to purchase the item. Nothing I'm referring to is nearly as personal to you as the destiny you birth. Your destiny is far more important and personal. How it's expressed to the world matters significantly!

From the moment we say *"yes"* to conception, we begin imagining our destiny. Like some young girl may fantasize about her wedding day, you begin dreaming of how your destiny will appear. No one imagines an insignificant company, a horrible song sounding, or an unread book. No one sits in the silence of the evening, cradling their swollen belly and visualizing their child as being hideously ugly.

How your child is expressed matters because we know that expression drives reception, and reception is always related to success. An unattractive business idea will struggle to gain support. An unappealing book will not gain readers. A mediocre song will not attract listeners. You desire your destiny to be a great success so expression matters!

The imagined expression of your destiny will rarely match the realized expression.

In the months and years leading up to this realization, your imagination created such a strong image of something unseen that you could have easily drawn a picture. You had never actually seen the product of your womb, but it usually feels like you have. The imagined expression of your destiny will rarely match the realized expression. Managing the gap is key to moving forward.

Jonathan and Nina Martinez are not only a great couple but wonderful friends. They were blessed with a son, Matthew, and a little while later discovered they would have a second child. Everything was progressing normally. Jonathan and Nina were already imagining life with their little baby and its big brother. Shock and panic set in when, approaching their delivery date, it was discovered in an ultrasound that their child would be born with a cleft palate. It was an emotional moment when, later that day, they were told that their baby was a girl. They named her Isabella.

The imagined life was suddenly replaced with reality. Isabella would potentially require several surgeries and special care just to be able to eat properly. They had imagined snuggling their daughter, not changing her dressing. They had imagined hearing the coos of a newborn, not the screams of a baby fighting medical procedures. Just before birth, medical technology brought a reality that reality didn't match their imagined existence.

Today, Isabella is almost through with her surgeries. The doctors have done amazing work. She is beautiful and happy. Jonathan and Nina wouldn't change anything, but there is no denying that the imagined expression was different than the reality. I'm impressed with how they managed the gap between imagination and reality.

No matter what image or situation your imagination creates, it will not be accurate. You may dream of a company that dominates the market and initially realize a company that struggles to get off the ground. Don't fall apart. Manage the gap!

The Reception Gap

The second gap is reception. Intentionally or not, you have a vision for how your baby will be received by others. As we stated earlier, success is often determined by the reception something or someone receives. Your imagination will likely paint a picture of others receiving your destiny with excitement and maybe a little bit of awe. You anticipate your announcement being met with smiles. You know everyone is going to want to hold your baby!

It is common for the business owner to picture the customers coming through the doors of their shop *"oohing"* and *"ahhing"* over the displays you have prepared. Resources have been poured into preparing for the moment your door opens for the first time.

The imagination sees crowds poised at the front door like it's Black Friday at a discount store and everything is seventy-five percent off! I pray that's the reality you experience on the first day, but it may not be. Your first customers may be fewer than imagined. Instead of *"oohing"* and *"ahhing"* over your products and displays, they may complain about your pricing and the setup of your store. You may experience a reception gap.

I can't imagine how Mary must have felt when she and Joseph arrived in Bethlehem. Making their way through the streets toward the inn, she probably imagined the soft bed, clean sheets, and quiet ambiance of a well-run establishment. She had traveled for days on the back of a donkey. The fact that she was about to deliver a child made the journey even more difficult. It would not have been unreasonable for her to imagine that the innkeeper would see her condition and quickly get them into a comfortable room. I am hypothesizing about what Mary thought, but it may not be a huge stretch.

When the innkeeper let them know that there was no room available and that they would be sleeping in the stable, I think a reception gap existed. In an agrarian society, close proximity to animals was not abnormal, but she was planning to stay in the inn. Can you imagine Mary's thoughts? Scripture doesn't share them with us. Maybe it's because we would struggle to accept her as the mother of Jesus if we knew what she was really thinking. My thoughts might have gone something like, *"I'm about to deliver a child. God is the Father of this baby. You'd think that if He could arrange a virgin birth, a nice bed wouldn't have been too hard! And the innkeeper! If he recognized who this baby was, he would kick everyone else out to make us comfortable."*

When imagining your child's reception by others, we rarely consider the possibility that their arrival may not be welcomed! Other than on airplanes, buses, or trains, social norms have not prepared us for the potential that some people don't want our baby around. That's the reality of the story I shared about calling the pastor of the established church in town. I thought he would greet our child with joy, but I was wrong. He looked at me like I was a mother of twins boarding a plane, and the seat next to him was the last one left! There was a gap in the reception experience.

The Maturation Gap

The third gap is maturation. This is the gap between how your destiny matures in your imagination and how it matures in reality. This gap includes how quickly things progress as you introduce your destiny to the world.

William was a charismatic entrepreneur who knew business was his destiny. His business launched strong and began to grow. For the first few years, sales were strong, but growth was slow. He had opportunities to rub shoulders with owners of far larger and more established companies. He began to see the experienced staff, the financial reserves, and the lifestyle of the executives. These were things William was not yet receiving from his business. His staff was young and small, and while they were working hard to develop reserves, the accounts were slim. His lifestyle wasn't much different than if he was working nine to five for someone else except that he carried the responsibility of ownership. Frustration set in. The thought dominating his life was, *"I thought this business would be further along by now."*

William is not alone.

Maturity is when something is able to maximize its potential. Most of us desire maturity long before it arrives. We imagine a destiny with big things happening quickly, with a sense of safety, comfort, and control. This is when the business is strong, has reserves in the bank, and offers the lifestyle the owners desire. It is when the ministry develops enough to be consistently achieving the vision it was created for. This is when the family is enjoying the benefits of being together and all the needs are met.

The reality is that most destinies take far longer to mature than planned. I think this is what we see Marry struggling with while attending a wedding in the town of Cana.[45] While Mary, Jesus, and his disciples were in attendance, the wedding began to run out of wine. Culturally speaking, this was a disaster for the hosts. Buying more wine was not an option and the situation was getting worse by the moment.

I don't know why a guest like Mary became involved in the process, but at some point, she became aware of the problem. While most people were thinking there was no hope for this situation, Mary was thinking something different. She brought the servants to Jesus and said to Him, *"They have no more wine."*

Jesus responded by saying, *"Dear woman, that's not our problem. My time has not yet come."* [46]

I'm going to read into this moment a little. Mary was pushing Jesus to do something He had never done before. She was asking Him to do a miracle to fix a problem. Jesus was telling her, *"no."* In my mind, Mary was dealing with a maturation gap. Jesus was thirty years old at this point. She knew His birth had been miraculous. She was a virgin when he was conceived, and she knew, more than anyone, that she had not slept with a man.

Gabriel had made some incredible statements about what her Son would accomplish. The angel said He would be called the Son of God. He said that Jesus would be great and that God would give Him the throne of David. The angel said that her son Jesus would reign over Israel forever and His kingdom would never end! These were huge statements, but as far as Mary could tell, at thirty, Jesus had only made a few friends. While these friends were nice enough – they were mostly fishermen. How they would help Jesus ascend to any throne was beyond her understanding. In short, I believe Mary was thinking, *"By now I thought we would be further along in the fulfillment of God's promise, but it really doesn't look like we've progressed far."*

We know that Mary spoke to the servants and said, *"Do whatever he tells you."* In my imagination, she then shot a hard, squinty-eyed glance at her son and walked away.

I think Mary was dealing with a maturation gap.

Don't Stop Now

These three gaps cause frustration and anxiety throughout the world as people deal with realities that don't align with their dreams. The perceived difference between the two can be frustrating, scary, and discouraging. I've experienced every one of these gaps and none of them are easy to navigate. If left alone, each gap will widen. If unaddressed, this space between what you hoped for, and what you see, can become so wide they seem unbridgeable. Many people stop at the gap.

Stopping here makes sense. We all know that businesses fail, families fall apart, churches dissolve, songs fade away, and relationships end. Such is the nature of life in a broken world. It makes sense to stop at the gap, and many do. Most people never make it to the realization of their destiny. They live within the hopes and dreams of others. Most folks choose to become observers, commentating on the successes and failures of those who are birthing destinies while leaving their own to die from lack of attention.

The issue is that there are no true spectators in life. We are all participants. The author of the book of the Bible called Hebrews wrote, *"Therefore we also, since we are surrounded by so great a cloud of witnesses, let us lay aside every weight, and the sin which so easily ensnares us, and let us run with endurance the race that is set before us, looking unto Jesus, the author and finisher of our faith, who for the joy that was set before Him endured the cross, despising the shame, and has sat down at the right hand of the throne of God."*[47]

You may notice that the words *"we," "us,"* and *"our"* are used a total of seven times. The author is writing to every reader both individually and collectively. He is also including himself in this description of life. By using the Greek terms translated *"we", "us",* and *"our,"* he is writing inclusively. Every person is running a race before them. It's run collectively in the sense that everyone is moving forward, progressing through life. No one can pause life to choose another track or change what has already occurred. Everyone is running. The race is run individually because no one can run another's race for them instead of their own.

I believe that the only true spectators of life are those who have already completed their race. Yes, I can observe you as you run, but I am also running. This means that the gaps we face are common to all of us and must be navigated – alone. These gaps can be overcome. Those who raise their destiny to maturity must manage the gaps! Thankfully, it is not beyond anyone's ability. Your destiny is depending on you!

CHAPTER 22

Managing the Gaps

Through the years, I've been privileged to walk beside people who have planted churches, built businesses, started families, recorded albums, and launched careers. Many other stories have been witnessed from farther away through friends, family, and the media. There has never been a destiny where gaps between the imagination and reality did not exist in some form.

In this chapter, we will make suggestions on how to manage these gaps. These suggestions are offered knowing that every situation is unique. What works in one may not be effective in another. The good news is that there are principles that, intentionally applied, can benefit any gap management issue.

In this chapter, I'll use the life of my sister and brother-in-law as an illustration. Kurt and Regan Sorenson have managed gaps better than almost anyone I know. Their story has inspired me as I've navigated the gaps in my own life.

Kurt and Regan have two sons. Regan's pregnancy was not easy with either, but eventually they were born. Troy, the oldest, has grown and developed into a strong, intelligent, and active boy. In many ways, Troy is advanced for his age. He is quick to understand concepts and has incredible verbal skills. Kaden, their second son, is also a bright and happy boy who, unlike

Troy, deals with a developmental disability. For years, his disability was attributed to a rare genetic anomaly, but at the time of this writing, geneticists have concluded that the genetic issue is benign, leaving his disability undiagnosed.

While it presents much like autism, he is not autistic. Kaden does not speak in words; he expresses himself through hand signals and verbal noises like grunts, groans, and squeals. While dealing with unique challenges, Kaden has developed into a sweet, happy boy who delights in the simplest things in life. I am blessed every time I have the privilege of connecting with him. Kurt and Reagan are incredible parents who have navigated gaps few of us will face.

Kaden was born premature and physical issues plagued his first months, creating a reality of hospital stays, consistent monitoring, and repeated testing. The day eventually arrived that the last liver test returned with good news, and the doctor gave the all clear for him to go home. It was a day of rejoicing! That rejoicing didn't last long. The moment the good report was received, Kaden began having seizures. The seizures led to further testing which revealed Kaden's ongoing disability.

This is not the life Kurt or Regan had imagined for their second son. The news rocked their world and immediately changed the trajectory of their future. Observing them navigating the gaps has been incredible, and they have given me permission to use their story to help you navigate the gaps in the realization of your destiny.

Addressing the Expression Gap

Let's begin by addressing the expression gap. Remember, the expression gap is how your offspring is expressed in the world. It encompasses the appearance, natural tendencies, and gifts of your baby. Your imagination offers a picture that reality has not managed to present.

You dreamed of a company that dominates the market, and your reality is that the company is struggling to get off the ground. Don't fall apart. Manage the gap!

Managing this gap begins during expectation. Waiting until the business launches to consider the possibility that everything won't go as planned is too late. Understand that the gap exists and be intentional from the beginning.

In Mary's life, the reality of Christ's birth was miraculous. There was no way she could have expected or understood how it occurred. She was in the process of a miracle from the first conversation.

> *No matter what image or situation your imagination creates, it will not be accurate.*

The process of birthing your destiny is likely to be overall less miraculous. You will know how conception occurred and be able to track your time of expectation. As you approach delivery, the nuts and bolts of launching a company, writing a book, or developing an idea will cause the practicalities to become prominent. It will feel and look like you have a solid handle on what is to come. During this time, intentionally focus on the fact that the reality of your destiny remains unknown. No matter what image or situation your imagination creates, it will not be accurate.

Managing the gap means intentionally creating a margin in your imagined outcome. If you're starting a business, prioritize your rollout plan. You may not have everything you dreamt of on day one. If writing a book, hope that a major publisher will promote your first novel, but consider that self-publishing to a smaller market may be the first expression of your vision. Create margin in your imagined expression.

Secondly, devote yourself to the vision and not the expression. Kurt and Regan knew the troubled pregnancy would likely create complications after birth, but they could not predict what reality would bring. When faced with it, they were shaken and uncertain, but they persevered. Their devotion to the vision was greater than their devotion to an expression.

The vision was to develop their family by raising healthy, well-adjusted children. They are doing exactly that. The expression of their vision may be different than what they expected, but their devotion never wavered. I've never heard them say, *"I wish Kaden was never born."* The expression was not as important as the vision.

Devotion to the vision allows you to adjust the expression. In a less emotional example, the expression of a song may change based on the quality of musicians available for recording. Lesser musicians may offer a simpler expression while more accomplished talent may add layers of musical depth. Dedication to the vision allows for adjustments to be made to the expression. The greatest impact will be made when your destiny moves into the world.

Addressing the Reception Gap

The second gap is the reception gap. Remember, intentionally or not, you have a vision for how your baby will be received by others. Regan shared a powerful story with me illustrating the reality of this gap and how to manage it.

For a long while, Regan and Kurt were determining what life would be like with a disabled child, negotiating their relationship with Kaden. The seizures were finally under control, and they had also received news that Kaden would not deal with them all his life. That was such a relief that the remaining reality of a developmental delay seemed relatively minor. Regan said, *"I never really thought about how others would receive Kaden. Kurt and I were just trying to learn how to receive him ourselves. It was then that we attended a conference for parents of children with disabilities. It was the worst experience I've had at a conference."*

During a group discussion, other parents began publicly sharing their experiences with their children. Several expressed frustration, anger, shame, and embarrassment regarding the reception others had for their disabled child. It was the first time Regan had considered this reality. It was a gap.

Some parents were angry because people ignored their child while others were frustrated that people looked at or attempted to interact with theirs. These expectations are entirely personal, and these parents have the right to expect whatever they would like. My commentary is not a judgment on the validity of their feelings, but on the reality of their situation. Regan realized that in the minds of some, the only way others could properly interact with their disabled child was entirely dependent on how the parent felt in that moment! It seemed like it was a no-win situation.

Regan's next words may help you manage the reception gap. *"I had not really considered how others would receive Kaden. In this moment, however, I realized that whatever my desires were, I could not determine how others would receive him."* She continued, *"I just assume everyone out there is going to think Kaden is as cute as I do. People are not bad. There are a lot of good people out there. They see a child with a disability and their ignorance of what is expected of them causes them to be afraid. They are not afraid of my son, but of making a mistake. Parents will stop their kids from playing with Kaden because they don't want them to hurt him. The reality is Kaden loves it when other kids play with him! The reception issue is rarely bad people, but limited knowledge of how to interact with someone with a disability or delay. My job is to open the door of opportunity as wide as possible. Their reception of Kaden has everything to do with the attitude Kurt and I take."*

I'm intentionally using a child with a disability to illustrate this point. Most people who have not been close to a disabled or delayed individual aren't familiar with what is proper or desired in these situations. Those who love the disabled person can become hyper protective. They want the child to both be engaged by the world around them and protected against negative experiences. The polarized sensitivities create gaps.

While the reception of your destiny may not be as sensitive, it is still incredibly sensitive to you. You will want others to be engaged in whatever you birth. Its very survival may depend on others becoming customers, readers, listeners, or promoters. Interaction is necessary, but it may be difficult to manage your expectations of their reception. The difficulty goes to the next level when those observing your destiny become critical, dismissive, or even offensive.

> *Settle the fact in your mind that some people will not like what you offer.*

The first step is recognizing that you will never be able to control others. Their thoughts and feelings are completely their own. Their preferences are not yours to demand. Settle the fact in your mind that some people will not like what you offer.

I'll never forget the first time a member of the church stopped attending. They were faithful for several months and seemed like they would be with us forever. Then one week, they were simply not there. It was easy to notice their disappearance because there were only ten or twelve people in the entire church! They didn't attend the next week, so I called them. Their statement floored me. *"We like you as a person. We just don't like you as our pastor."*

This cut me to the core. Their reception of me had been so favorable that they began attending. I assumed their appreciation would naturally extend to the destiny I was delivering. It didn't.

I was hurt that day, but I also learned a valuable lesson. I cannot control the reception others have of me. It was then that I became grateful for all those who attended weekly, allowing the ministry team and me to have influence in their lives. I embraced the reality that I will never control how others receive what I offer.

Secondly, take advantage of every opportunity to influence their reception. You cannot control anything, but you have many opportunities to influence. When Kurt and Regan assume that people will receive Kaden appropriately, it gives them an influential position. If someone takes a moment to interact with Kaden, but seems uncomfortable, they spend time introducing them to their son. Regan has a standard speech, *"This is Kaden Wade. He has a developmental delay. He is kind, sweet, and very happy. If you would like me to save you from him, I'll do it. If you'd like to get to know him, he would love that!"*

To date, only one person has refused to get to know Kaden. I say they missed an opportunity to get to know an incredible boy!

Kurt and Regan take the opportunity to influence the relationship. If I was talking about a business, I would call them the Kaden Inc. Sales Team. When others view your destiny with some level of concern, refuse the temptation to become angry, defensive, or aggressive. Instead, influence the situation! Let Regan's statement become your guide. *"This is (insert your destiny here). It is a (insert description here). If you would like me to save you from it, I'll be happy to do so. If you'd like to get to know a little more about it however, I'd love to introduce you!"*

Run through that a few times out loud. Get the concept in your mind. Managing the reception gap means intentionally engaging the audience. The audience is whoever is paying attention to your destiny. You can't control what they think or feel, but you can influence them.

There is one similarity between the reception to Kaden, our ministry, or your destiny: Gaining the attention of someone who doesn't want to be there is worse than not having them there at all! If their reception is negative and you can't influence them into becoming positive, it is better for everyone that they move on.

Addressing the Maturation Gap

The third obstacle is the maturation gap. This stands between how your destiny matures in your imagination compared to reality. This gap includes how quickly things progress as you introduce your destiny to the world.

We have said from the beginning of this book that what God is bringing forth from your life is completely unique. That's an easy statement to agree with until you are looking for a template to follow or a model to observe to plot our course forward. We search out stories of others realizing similar destinies to assess our progress. This happens in every area of life.

The church leader looks to churches around them to see if what they are experiencing is common or if something unique is happening. Parents watch children roughly the same age as theirs to see if their child is keeping up with their age group. Business leaders examine businesses around them to determine if their progress is what it should be in comparison to others.

When we first went to Kona, a well-meaning pastor met with me and said, *"Launching a church here will be difficult. You will likely never be a full-time pastor. My suggestion is to get a good job or start a business."* He was correct in saying it would be difficult, but wrong about full-time ministry. We were full-time pastors within two years.

Step one to managing the maturation gap is truly accepting that every destiny is unique. Yes, there will be similarities, but the success, failure, or viability of your destiny is not determined by the destiny of others.

The man expressing that being a full-time pastor in Hawaii would be impossible was not aware of the unique nature of my destiny. He was assuming his need for a second job while pastoring a church would also become my reality. His comment was meant to benefit me, but it proved incorrect.

Your destiny is completely unique in creation and maturation. I've watched as Kurt and Regan have raised Troy who is advanced in some ways and Kaden who is delayed in development. The Sorensons have many friends, but to my knowledge, they have never compared their sons' maturation rates to that of their friend's children. They have allowed their sons to mature according to their creation and accepted that they are completely unique.

A second technique to manage maturation gaps is striving for excellence instead of perfection. Perfection is an unachievable standard, but excellence presents the best version of your destiny possible. No one is perfect, but excellence is achievable by everyone.

A few days ago, Kaden expressed himself in a new way. He was sitting on Regan's bed before going to school when he pointed at himself then pointed at the bed. He was telling Regan that he wanted to go back to bed. For most children, this would not be remarkable, but for Kaden this was excellent! This was a level of self-awareness that he had not previously expressed.

Judging your destiny by levels of excellence instead of perfection allows you to accommodate its uniqueness.

Asking for perfection would be requiring something from Kaden that the most brilliant minds and incredible athletes of our day could not achieve. Expecting excellence from Kaden is possible. Excellence celebrates his achievements based on his abilities.

Judging your destiny by levels of excellence instead of perfection allows you to accommodate its uniqueness. It means expecting the best from your destiny within the context of its realities.

Excellence provided by a high school drama class will be different than that provided by a Broadway production. Excellence from a start-up will be different than that of an established business. Excellence from a new author isn't the same as that of an accomplished novelist. Striving for perfection will result in disappointment and frustration. Striving for excellence results in many opportunities for success!

The gaps between imagination and reality are ubiquitous. There is no escaping this component of realizing your destiny, but you can manage the gaps. Intentionally doing so is one of the great differences between those who raise their destiny into maturity and those whose dreams die before they've had a chance to live.

Your God-given destiny is meant to thrive! There is purpose behind God's creation. He is empowering you to experience the fulfillment of that purpose!

CHAPTER 23

The Slow Rollout

Facebook, Instagram, Snapchat, FaceTime, texting, and other instant communication tools make the slow rollout of information uncommon. You can reveal almost anything to your world of friends and family within seconds of it occurring, and if that's too long, some people choose to stream their lives in real time!

While sharing news and information can happen in a moment, the realization that your destiny has been delivered usually takes time. Remember, realization means to become fully aware of something, to cause something to happen, and to give physical form to something. You have caused something to happen, giving physical form to your destiny. Your baby is living and breathing. The rest of the world doesn't know it exists, but that's not their fault. This realization has not yet come to the world. The process of realization is unique to say the least.

In chapter thirteen, I shared how Tyrian was almost delivered on a Chicago highway. As exciting as that would've been, I'm thankful that he wasn't! He was born early in the morning on November 22, 2001. That day also happened to be Thanksgiving Day. Over the years, I've often felt bad for Tyrian because the family forgets his birthday. Everyone remembers he was born on

Thanksgiving, but that date changes every year! He has received gifts a week early, but more often, they arrive a week late.

Soon after Tyrian's delivery, Kristy settled into a nice bed in a comfortable room. The hospital was great and the nurses were helpful--too helpful. Every thirty minutes or so, a nurse would enter the room to check on Kristy and Tyrian. Being woken up for medical reasons is understandable, but stopping by to simply ask if everyone was ok left Kristy feeling crankier and crankier. Her patience ran out when a nurse walked into the room around six AM and asked if anyone wanted a newspaper.

After delivering Tyrian into the world just after midnight, the last thing Kristy wanted was a newspaper at six in the morning! She couldn't take it anymore. She turned to me and said, *"I want to go home!"* About an hour later, we made our way to the front door of the hospital, strapped our newborn into the car seat, and made the drive to our basement apartment. Sleeping in our own bed was wonderful.

The sleep, though good, came in spurts. Talon was two years old and Tyrian was hungry. We eventually remembered that it was Thanksgiving and we'd been invited to dinner by the Yonts family. In our time in Chicago, no one treated us more kindly than Jack and Jo Ann Yonts. They, along with their family, welcomed us to the area with open arms. They loved us and supported the church's launch. Until Tyrian's arrival, we had been looking forward to spending Thanksgiving with them.

My intention was to call them and politely cancel. We had a good excuse. Kristy had other ideas. *"We still have to eat,"* she said. So we packed up and went to lunch. We stood on their doorstep and rang the doorbell. While I don't remember who answered, I do recall that we were inside and greeting everyone before someone said, *"Hey! You have a baby with you! When was he born?"* Kristy answered, *"Twelve hours ago."*

That was the first moment someone other than Kristy, me, or the medical staff realized that our destiny had arrived. In that instant, they became fully aware. They didn't know everything we knew about him, that he had almost been born on the highway, or Kristy's interrupted sleep. They didn't have a vision for his future or know his name, but they knew he existed. They could see him, touch him, speak to him, and hold him. Tyrian was here and all the potential for what he could become existed within that tiny body.

From the moment of delivery, your destiny holds the potential for everything it can become.

From the moment of delivery, your destiny holds the potential for everything it can become. It exists as a ball of pure potential that has yet to be realized. It could be great, but it isn't yet. Think of it like the seed of a great sequoia tree. Nothing is added to the internal part of the seed after it settles into the soil. No one adds additional DNA markers into its genetic makeup or determines its growth potential once the seed has broken its protective shell. The seed itself contains the potential for everything that tree will ever become.

The seed will crack, and the seedling will begin to develop roots. Those roots will draw in nutrients from the outside to the tree, helping it develop and grow. A stem will make its way to the surface where leaves will develop. Those leaves will again draw resources from the world around into the tree. As this process occurs, the tree is being realized. The soil recognizes that resources are being pulled from its depths. The sun recognizes that its vitamins are being absorbed into the tree's leaves. The birds soon realize a new condo complex is being built. Seeing the tree's growth, hikers stop to admire the little tree that will one day soar above them, or more likely, their grandchildren. In time, all those who must know of its existence, know. The mighty tree stands tall and strong. It takes years for it to fully grow, but it is realized long before then. Your destiny is no different.

Realization has a natural progression, a process through which whatever you've birthed will be recognized, resourced, and then utilized by the outside world. The life of Jesus is a great example of this. Scripture describes Him as being the *"Lamb slain before the foundation of the world."* [48] This reveals that a plan, a process, and potential existed long before realization. With His infinite knowledge, God knew that Adam and Eve would refuse His guidance. God was unwilling to be separated from His creation forever, so He developed a plan to give humanity a choice. Before God created the Earth, a plan for Jesus to be born, live a perfect life, then die for humanity's sins was put into place. Jesus knew his destiny was to pay the price for sin through sacrifice. His purpose was clear, and He was ready to complete it.

You Were Created with a Destiny

This narrative reality excites me. If Jesus was born with everything necessary to fulfill His destiny, then so are you! We read God's words to the prophet Jeremiah encouraging him to give birth to his destiny, that he could make it through the process. God knew Jeremiah could birth his destiny because God created him for that purpose. Jeremiah's creation was intentional. God said, *"I knew you before I formed you in your mother's womb. Before you were born I set you apart and appointed you as my prophet to the nations."* [49]

Every language is unique. The original Hebrew language is complex to the English speaker. Words and phrases can have simultaneous multiple meanings. This brings a depth, breath, and beauty to the text that is often missed by the English-speaking reader.

In this case, God is saying that He knew Jeremiah before Jeremiah had a physical body. He created Jeremiah within his mother's womb and designed him with a specific destiny in mind: to become a prophet to the nations. This is where the Hebrew becomes unique. The translated word "appointed "[50] indicates that God gave Jeremiah to Israel as a prophet. He was designed to become a prophet; this was God's will, but it was also Jeremiah's choice. Jeremiah could have chosen to walk another path.

In the process of realizing a destiny, there is always a choice to be made by both the one birthing destiny and the one receiving it. We see these choices revealed in the life of Jesus as he made His way toward the cross. Jesus knew He was created for sacrifice. He told His disciples that the time for His departure from Earth was nearing. He then went to a garden or park called the Garden of Gethsemane. There, afraid and stressed, Jesus asked God if there was another way to accomplish the goal. This was when Jesus uttered the famous phrase, *"Father, if it is Your will, take this cup away from Me; nevertheless not My will, but Yours, be done."*[51] Jesus separated His will from His Father's will. The will of Jesus was to find another way. The will of the Father was to move forward with the plan that was established before the Earth was formed. Jesus was born for this purpose. This was His destiny. From birth, everything necessary for Him to achieve this goal was within Him, but He still had to choose to realize His destiny. The job of those He left behind was to help the world realize Jesus as Savior. Today, while most of the world knows about Him, sadly, many have yet to realize the power of His sacrifice. It is only by making the choice to follow Jesus that the reality of who He is can be fully realized in an individual life. I encourage you to accept Him as the Savior of your life. You may realize that He is everything He claimed to be!

Heaven Knows First

Notice where the realization of destiny began in the lives of both Jesus and Jeremiah. Throughout this book, I've talked about giving birth to a God-designed destiny. If this is the case, then Heaven knows about your destiny. A God-designed destiny always includes Heaven.

We live in a spiritually sensitive time. Many Christians and non-Christians alike are aware of spiritual signs and indicators. This is not a book on spiritual signs or signals. There is one particular signal, however, that Christians, mystics, and secularists all point to when destiny is being realized. The common phrase is, *"I was born to do this."* Someone from the outside will say, *"They were born to do that."* Obviously, something in that individual connects uniquely to their current situation. They could do something else, but they would never connect with that pursuit in the manner as this one. You know when you connect uniquely to something.

Heaven knows about your destiny.

I believe that this is Heaven's realization being revealed. In the life of Jesus, Heaven provided signs of His birth. A star shone above the place He was born, and a choir of angels sang to shepherds about His birth. These signs were Heaven's way of saying, *"Hey! Look at this. Recognize who has arrived!"*

As your destiny is realized, signs and signals will become evident. You may become anxious trying to find these signs. Relax! Everything will become clear in time. Heaven will naturally point the way. Trust God. Clarity will arrive.

For years, I tried to find something else to do besides pastoring and building churches. Frankly, there are easier ways to make a living. The uncertainties and uniquenesses of what I do can be overwhelming at times. The reality is that I've never found peace, happiness, or fulfillment doing anything else. I discovered what I was born to do. You will too!

You may think it's obvious that Heaven is aware when someone is called to be a pastor. However, the idea that Heaven cares if someone is designed to be a carpenter, business person, or entertainer may not be as obvious. I believe Heaven knows those realities as well.

Mario is a great friend who I had the privilege of pastoring in Kona, Hawaii. He and his wife, Naomi, were some of the first people to attend Legacy when we arrived. Mario is a great husband, father, and a master when it comes to working with drywall. I hung drywall for a little while, so I know how tough it can be, but Mario makes it look easy. When we were building the church in Kona, we'd hang drywall and then Mario would make it look good! Sometimes this meant redoing it completely! When handling drywall, or general carpentry, Mario is fast, certain, and consistent. He is born to work with his hands.

Heaven is not surprised by this revelation.

You Know Second

The bearer is second in line to realize the potential of their destiny. Mary understood from the beginning that her destiny would not be like any other. She knew as she made the transition from being His shelter to His supporter that the destiny she birthed was greater than herself.

This was clear when the shepherds arrived talking about how the angels sang of the Christ Child's arrival. It was clear years later when the wise men from the far east arrived at their home to worship and present gifts to Jesus. Mary wasn't pushing Jesus into the world, but the world was finding Him. The world was waking up to the realization that Mary was already living in.

You will be the second to recognize the potential in your God-designed destiny. As it dawns on you, excitement will build. Your knowledge will push you to pursue every possible area of development. Parents often see potential in their children and begin pushing them to realize it. Kids today are involved in sports, music lessons, school clubs, scouts, and many other activities in the attempt to discover or awaken potential.

It is interesting to think that Mary knew Jesus's potential before He understood it Himself before He even knew His own name. As God, He was completely aware, but His natural body hadn't caught up yet. So while nursing her son, Mary would dream of what He would become.

The challenge is knowing that potential exists, but not rushing the process. Remember, you are a steward of what God has placed within you. To guide its development, you must see the potential, but rushing the process could destroy the very thing you are trying to protect.

You are a steward of what God has placed within you.

Matthew had a gift. He was intelligent and quick to understand concepts. As a young boy, Matt's potential was evident. When opportunities to act out his gifts arose, he was often called upon. Being gifted, Matt could enjoy the blessings and benefits of these opportunities without exerting much effort.

Matt's parents were his greatest supporters. They told everyone about his potential and what he was doing. For years, he rose to the top of every list, and it looked like there were no limits to where he could go. Then things began to change. As Matthew grew, he encountered others who could do what he could do. Some of them had developed slower, but they had eventually arrived. Most of them had to work harder, but they eventually made it. Matt was no longer in a league of his own. His advanced development at a young age had caused him to be unique, but he was beginning to slide toward average.

As this was happening, his parents began explaining away the change in opportunities. They blamed others for not accepting their son. They saw imaginary plots to sabotage his rise to greatness. Eventually, they blamed everything and everyone except for the true reason behind Matt's eventual failures. His potential was realized quickly and introduced to the world. He was unique in youth and was given a platform he didn't earn. Matt never learned the value of hard work and diligence. With those two elements, he could have risen to greatness. Without them, he slid from mediocrity to obscurity.

In their zeal to make Matt's potential known, they pushed him quickly into the world. They thought they were loving him by neglecting to hold him accountable for his actions and lack of work ethic, but it was damaging. Ultimately, they hurt the one they were trying desperately to protect.

You will recognize the potential of your destiny long before others, but allow the process to take place. It seems easier to push your destiny out into the world, but it's better to allow realization to occur at the proper time.

Others Know Last

The shepherds were third in realizing that the Christ Child had been born. They were common men. They were good people with open hearts. They were humble enough to receive the words of the angels and bold enough to seek out Christ, but they were not people of influence. I'm using the term *"common"* to indicate those who are good, moral and ethical people who are inherently important but lack a large amount of influence.

The dream is for your destiny's potential to be realized by someone who can catapult you forward. It is the singer's dream to be discovered by Simon Cowell or to make their debut on the latest television competition show. However, the common person will often see the potential first. Jesus' potential being recognized by shepherds was like a singer being loved by a few people in a small church in rural America. It's great to hear, and wonderful to experience the love, but their approval can't help the singer break into Nashville. This level of realization will not catapult your destiny forward, but it is a necessary part of the process.

In my mind, this is the real life equivalent of Jesus saying, *"If you are faithful in little things, you will be faithful in large ones. But if you are dishonest in little things, you won't be honest with greater responsibilities."*[52] I've had the privilege of meeting a few famous people. All of them handled their moment on stage quite well. The ones that made the biggest impact on my life, however, were those who were faithful in managing our personal interaction properly. If you asked any of them if they remembered meeting me, they would truthfully say, *"No."* But when we met, they made the effort to make our interaction important.

Treating people honorably will always be right.

Take careful note of this point. How you treat the common person who realizes the potential of your destiny will have a direct impact on your further development. Their support alone may not change your life, but there are far more *"common people"* than people of great influence. Treating people honorably will always be right. Make the time to appreciate everyone involved in the realization of your destiny. It is only after enough common people connect with your destiny that anyone else will take notice.

Approximately three years after His birth, Jesus was recognized by Magi from the far east. They had seen signs in the stars that someone special, a king, would be born in the area. They traveled a long way to see this new king, and when they arrived in Jerusalem, they caused a stir and eventually made their way to the palace for an audience with the king. While the shepherds had known about Jesus for years, King Herod was still ignorant of His existence.

It will take time for people of influence to realize the potential of your destiny. Understand that the more influential a person becomes, the more opportunities they receive. The common person seeks opportunities and usually takes any. The influential person spends more time sorting out the opportunities that have sought them in order to focus on the right ones. Let the process unfold in your life.

We don't know whether anyone recognized Jesus's potential between the shepherd's visit and the wise men's arrival. Mary could have become frustrated and angry at the slow progress, but it's more likely that she was enjoying the time with her baby.

I encourage you to enjoy the time with your baby. It may be slow going right now, but your destiny will develop quickly. When maturity arrives, you will think back on these moments just as parents reminisce as their adult children leave home. Adulthood will arrive fast enough. Enjoy these beautiful moments with your baby.

You will recognize the wise men by the bridge they create. They may live far away and may not be influential themselves, but they provide a bridge to those who are influential. This may be someone who lacks personal influence but roomed with a leader in your industry in college. It could be someone from out of town who helped you connect with someone influential. The fact is that you will rarely know who this person is unless they reveal themselves.

In my life, everyone is a wise person. Many people see a church on television and think that is what made them successful. That thought is often incorrect. Yes, mass media will cause a church to be more well-known and recognized, but most of a church's growth and development is done through relationships. One person reaches out to another and extends an introduction. I encourage you to greatly respect everyone who shows interest in your destiny. You don't know what part they will play in helping it mature.

Eventually, a key relationship will be established. When the Magi arrived, things began to change. Until their arrival, the life of Mary, Joseph, and Jesus remained much the same...except with a baby. After the Magi's visit, decisions were going to be made that would change life forever.

Once the influencers become aware of your destiny's potential, things pick up. The pace shifts. I hope you have your seatbelt fastened. In the next chapter, our rollout will continue!

CHAPTER 24

Defined by Your Destiny

The Magi traveled to worship. With palpable excitement, they arrived at Herod's palace. The signs from the heavens told them that no normal king would be born in this region, so they traveled from far away for around three years to bring gifts.

Most scholars believe that the stars gave the signs of Jesus' birth. It was then that they would have noticed, gathered their necessities, and began the long journey to find the one they described as King of the Jews. When they arrived in Jerusalem, they began asking if anyone knew where this king was.

These influential people took notice of Mary's destiny. They recognized the signs of potential from far away and made their way toward the source. This unique time in the development of a destiny is different in every situation. For a company, it may look like an order for product from an uncultivated client. For an artist, it might be an invitation to perform in a new venue. For an author, it could be an unsolicited speaking engagement. In each case, someone of influence will begin making noise about what they see connected to your destiny.

This exciting time can also be dangerous. The Magi carried influence with them, and their questions caused Herod to hear of Jesus for the first time. The Roman Empire had placed Herod in Jerusalem as king. His job was to rule Israel and ensure their allegiance to Rome. He had a lot of power and that power was able to be passed on to his children. He did not want to lose his authority. It also bothered him that the Magi were calling this child *"the King of the Jews"* while Herod was the one sitting on the throne. There was no way he was going to allow this to pass unanswered.

Herod called his advisors and asked where the Christ was to be born. Quoting the Old Testament prophet Micah, they informed Herod that the Christ would be born in Bethlehem. Armed with this knowledge, Herod called for an audience with the Magi and directed them to let him know once the child was found. He professed his intention to worship, but in reality, Herod wanted to destroy what he saw as his competition.

Competition

In the birth and development of your destiny, you are creating a threat to the powers that currently exist. When launching a new business, writing a new song, authoring a book, or even starting a family, you must be aware of the competition. Your offering will begin competing for the attention of the potential audience, and your competition won't always like it.

While my sister Regan and I were growing up, we were the best of friends. Her brilliance caused her to skip a grade and, being only fourteen months apart, this allowed us to go through school together. Regan and I were constantly in each other's life. We were best friends. Throughout our teenage years, we talked about every aspect of life, including who we were dating. While neither of us always wholeheartedly approved of the other's choice, our selection of dates never became an issue between us. That is until I became serious about possibly marrying Kristy.

As my relationship with Kristy moved forward, I noticed that Regan and I were not doing well. Soon, I realized that while Regan had always liked Kristy, she was becoming increasingly critical of this girl I was growing to love. One day, I went to Regan's room and confronted her. After a few moments of avoiding the issue, she finally blurted out, *"You don't get that while you are gaining a wife, I am losing my best friend!"*

There was nothing wrong with my connection to Kristy. Regan wanted me to be happy and have a great marriage. It was also unintentionally creating an area of competition for my attention. Regan knew that the closer Kristy and I became, the further away from her I would become. While she and I remain close to this day, our relationship shifted dramatically from what it once was. The effect was unintended, but very real.

Even in the best situation, your destiny will be a threat to something. Everyone celebrates the arrival of a new baby, but the older sibling recognizes they will be getting less attention. The lifelong friends of the new parents are happy, but also annoyed that their friends are no longer available to hang out several nights a week. No one is directly upset at the new baby, but its arrival threatens some part of their life. If the new baby could exist and everything stay exactly the same, everyone would be just fine. That never happens.

A new business impacts market share. A new church gives one more choice to a community of worshipers. A new book competes for shelf space. No matter how the destiny looks, it will impact the current understanding of what is normal. No one is completely ok with their normal being shifted.

When influencers begin to make noise about your destiny, your Herod will rise up. Herod's declaration was, *"I want to worship also."* In reality, Herod only wanted to destroy the threat. When he realized the Magi were not going to help him identify the young king, he decided to kill all the baby boys in the area who were two years old or younger!

Joseph was warned that something terrible was about to happen, so he packed up his family and fled to Egypt. Mary, Joseph, and Jesus lived in Egypt until it was safe to go back home. From Egypt, they returned home to Nazareth where Jesus grew to adulthood.

Your reality probably won't involve packing up your family and fleeing to another country. The survival of your destiny will probably not necessitate avoiding a dictator bent on destruction, but there will be Herods to deal with. Accept that and ready yourself for the challenge.

This book is less about crafting your destiny and more about being healthy through the process.

We tend to respond negatively toward Herod. It's terrible that he would kill all those children to save his own kingdom, but what would you do if you were in his shoes?

This book is less about crafting your destiny and more about being healthy through the process. It is about birthing your destiny. I didn't think much about Herod's point of view for many years. Like most, I read the story and judged him terribly for wanting to destroy Jesus and being willing to kill so many others in the process. Then I heard about a new church launching in Kona.

I don't remember who shared that a new startup church was launching, but I do remember the negative emotions. Legacy was doing well. We were growing into a healthy, strong, and well-rounded church. We were having a good time, but this news affected me. I wish I could tell you that I welcomed it. I wish I could share that I thought only of the people who would come to know Jesus through this new church, but I can't. My first thought was, *"How is this new church going to hurt Legacy?"*

Over time, I learned that the new pastor had built a team from the mainland. They had all moved to Kona to launch this church together. The more I heard, the more dismissive I became. While I never outright attacked them or their cause, I doubted their purpose and their future. These criticisms were not shared openly, but they existed. In weaker moments, I heard myself expressing them to others.

Soon, I heard that they had launched services and were having some success. The more they succeeded, the more I was frustrated with them and the more open I became with my criticisms. Remember the story I shared with you about the pastor who seemed to be actively working against us? At some point, I realized that I was doing the same thing. While my words and actions were different, the spirit and attitude were the same.

That revelation devastated me. I began asking God's forgiveness and attempting to determine the origin of these negative attitudes. The answer was clear. I was afraid. I was afraid that after the long years spent trying to survive, we were just going to fight another battle. I was afraid that this new church would become competition for the attention of Legacy's believers. The reality was that I was afraid for the survival of my destiny.

This is when my thoughts about Herod shifted. What he did was obviously inexcusably wrong, but why he acted is understandable. He was already sitting on the throne. This new king had just been born, and he would not only be a threat to his throne, but also to the throne of his son and grandsons. Herod was working to protect his destiny!

A God-designed destiny will not need to be afraid of the destiny of others.

I would do almost anything in my power to protect my sons and help them succeed. In Herod's case, destroying their competition was within his power and even generally accepted and understood during his time. He was doing what most fathers would have done.

The leaders of this new church were not working against Legacy; they were trying to bring forth their own destiny. I never met them personally, but this revelation shook me to my core. I realized that fear for my destiny was overpowering my faith that God was in charge of the future. It changed my prayers. I began praying for God to bless that new church and protect their leadership team. When a few people from Legacy decided to begin attending that church, we blessed them. To my knowledge, the new church is doing well. Legacy is also thriving. A God-designed destiny will not need to be afraid of the destiny of others.

Those who stand against your destiny will rarely do so because of personal animosity toward you. People will threaten your destiny because of how it affects them. They are afraid of how you will change their reality. While the change you bring may be unintentional, it will be real. Understanding this will help navigate these new waters. I pray that you will remember these moments in years to come when you are on their side of the equation.

Until then, celebrate. When influencers begin to attack your destiny, you know that it's now on the map. You are now something and someone to be acknowledged and addressed, and your destiny is now being recognized and realized.

Self-Realization

Heaven will be the first to realize the potential of your destiny. You will be the second. Third will be those who lack influence, followed by those with limited influence. These people will introduce your destiny to others with greater influence. The next realization will come to your destiny itself. At some point, Jesus realized His own potential. I will skim over a few realizations that will occur after this, but the moment of self-realization is key to the long-term viability of your destiny.

We can't say for certain exactly when self-realization occurred, but we can surmise that it was when Jesus was around twelve years old. Every year, the family traveled from Nazareth to Jerusalem for Passover celebrations. Those days, traveling could be dangerous, so people often traveled in groups. After celebrations, and while they were headed home, Mary and Joseph realized that Jesus wasn't with them. They thought He was traveling with others in their party, but in fact He had been left behind!

They raced back to Jerusalem to find their son sitting in the temple. He was in the middle of all the teachers who normally gave the talks. At twelve years old, Jesus was discussing the Law and the Prophets with the most educated minds of the day. They were shocked! Getting His attention, Mary said, *"Son, why have You done this to us? Look, Your father and I have sought You anxiously."* [53]

Jesus said, *"Why did you seek Me? Did you not know that I must be about My Father's business?"* [54] Notice that Mary used the word father to indicate Joseph. When Jesus used the word Father, it was to indicate someone connected to the temple. At some point, Jesus had begun realizing His own potential. He knew who He was, and He began acting on what He knew.

This concept is a little more ethereal when dealing with birthing what seems to be an inanimate destiny. A child can obviously experience self-realization. The observer can see joy and excitement when the baby first puts together that the object waving wildly in front of their face is their hand. Watching kids discover their own wills, their own dreams, and their own strengths is something every parent understands. What about those who are birthing something that cannot experience self-realization, such as a book or a song?

These things may be the expression of your destiny, but they are not the destiny itself. You are the one impacting the world with the expression of your destiny. If that's inanimate, then it will never have a moment of self-realization. Your destiny, however, will begin operating independently. This is a form of realizing the potential of itself.

I am a pastor. My destiny is to impact the world through building and developing the local church. I've shared many stories about the building of Legacy Church in Kona. A church is not an inanimate object; it has a life of its own. Kristy and I saw clearly when the church began to realize its own potential. It began with a simple Christmas Parade float.

Every Christmas, Kona hosts a parade. It is a time of celebration, creativity, and music. The first few years that Legacy was involved, Kristy and I led the charge. We organized the efforts, pushed the vision, and worked hard to help build the float. Then, one year, things shifted.

The moment your destiny begins influencing your time and attention more than you are influencing its time and attention, self-realization has begun.

As the time of the parade approached, we decided we would take a break from participation. It was a lot a work and our attention was needed elsewhere in the church's development. We weren't going to worry about it, but then a group of people came to us and said, *"It's time to get going on the Christmas float."* When we told them we weren't going to be involved that year, they responded, *"How about if we take it and make it happen. You just show up to the parade!"*

This was the first time I can remember that what we had birthed was making the plans for us. We were always pushing, pulling, and working hard to get the church to move. Now, it was telling us to move! We agreed, and the event went off without a hitch.

The moment your destiny begins influencing your time and attention more than you are influencing its time and attention, self-realization has begun.

In your life, the names will be different, but the realities will be the same. Your destiny will begin influencing your time and attention. Until they found Jesus in the temple, Mary and Joseph had determined when and where He would be. He may have waited for them, but they were never looking for Him. A change had occurred. Jesus had realized His own potential, and nothing would ever be the same.

This is exciting because self-realization marks when your destiny begins to live outside of you and function largely on its own. It could accomplish its mission without you if it had to. Mary and Joseph had raised Jesus, but once He knew who His Father was, Mary's destiny could be accomplished without her.

Over time, others would begin realizing Jesus's potential. John the Baptist would recognize Him and announce His presence to the world. Jesus had waited until he was mature to begin calling for disciples when He was thirty. Once these close followers were developed, then the crowds began to realize His potential. In fact, the potential of Jesus is still being realized today. Many years after His death, burial, and resurrection, the realization of Jesus continues!

There are more followers of Christ today than ever before. Mary's destiny has far outlived her. In fact, Mary is identified almost exclusively by her destiny. One may mention the name Mary and be asked, *"Which Mary are you speaking of?"* If the same person said, *"Jesus' mother,"* there would be no questions. Initially, she defined her destiny, but eventually her destiny defined her.

As your destiny continues to develop, many more will realize its potential. For some, like Mary, your destiny will eventually define you. Bill Gates is forever defined by Microsoft. Steve Jobs can't be separated from Apple. You will become defined by the destiny you birth, but you will also live outside of your destiny, just like Mary.

CHAPTER 25

Living in Destiny

Realization is the final process of delivering your destiny. The final part of the realization process is the transition from controlling your destiny to living within it and allowing it to operate at its full potential.

A God-designed destiny will always be greater than the one who bore it. Mary is a great example of this reality. Her destiny was to give birth to a baby that was the Son of God. He was God wrapped in flesh. This reality was greater than Mary could ever truly understand. While your destiny will not contain the same elements as Mary's, it will develop to become greater than yourself.

Everyone must eventually allow their destiny to soar, but there will also be tension between control and growth. If you allow your destiny to grow into its potential, then you must relinquish greater amounts of control. If you try to control it, your destiny will never achieve all that it could. The sad reality is that you cannot have both. For actual potential to be reached, your destiny must become greater than you.

If your business does not grow, it won't provide the life you desire and will not last beyond you. The family must become greater than you, or it will die when you die. The church must become greater than you, or it will only impact a few people. Your book should become greater than you by gaining more readers than just the people you personally know. No matter what the destiny looks like, a God-designed destiny will be greater than the one who gave it life.

At the wedding in the village of Cana, Mary had to push Jesus into performing a miracle. This stage didn't last long. Jesus was soon doing miracles in places Mary had never been. Before long, His name was known by more people than she would ever meet. Ultimately, He would launch a movement that demonstrated His miraculous power. In a reality that Mary could have never imagined, Jesus is still doing miracles today!

Making this transition means learning to live within your destiny instead of outside it.

As our sons are growing up, Kristy and I are intentionally transitioning our relationship with them. We recognize that a change is going to occur whether we like it or not. They are becoming young men. They will soon develop careers, fall in love, get married, and develop lives of their own. We're transitioning our relationship now, rather than by necessity later. At the time of this writing, we don't know how this is going to turn out. We do believe that it will be better to intentionally shift toward living with young men than trying to keep our boys at home.

I'd rather live within my sons' adult lives without the ability to control everything than outside of it wishing I played a part.

Every parent of adult children will recognize the difference. It means entertaining ideas from our children that Kristy and I didn't come up with. It means allowing them to make choices we wouldn't. It means talking through decisions instead of commanding them. It is a different mentality, but we pray that it will allow us to maintain a strong bond through the shift. I'd rather live within my sons' adult lives without the ability to control everything than outside of it wishing I played a part.

Mary conceived, birthed, and raised Jesus, and then sent Him into the world. I can't imagine what she experienced as she watched her Son navigate life as the Savior. My heart and mind can't comprehend what she felt as Jesus was nailed to the cross. I'm overwhelmed thinking of the joy she must have experienced seeing her Son resurrected after three days. She then watched Him rise to the Heavens. For that experience, I have no words.

The greatest illustration of someone transitioning to living within their destiny is that of Mary in the upstairs room with the rest of the disciples during the feast of Pentecost. Before Jesus was taken into Heaven, He told everyone to go to Jerusalem and wait for the promise of the Father. God had said that the Holy Spirit would come when Jesus was gone from the Earth. It would make sense for Mary to think, *"I've done my part. I conceived, expected, delivered, and realized Jesus. My part is done."* But Mary wasn't ready to be an onlooker in the unfolding story of her destiny, so she made her way to the room in Jerusalem with one hundred and twenty other believers. It was in that room that the Holy Spirit introduced Himself and began living inside each believer.

Until this time, the Kingdom of God was expressed on Earth through Jesus. Now it was being expressed in the lives of each believer. Mary's destiny was to deliver the Christ Child. Her destiny outgrew her and rather than walking away to observe it from the outside, Mary chose to live within the Kingdom created by her destiny.

How to Transition

You will not be miraculously filled with the presence of the destiny you birthed. You will absolutely have to make a choice. The obvious question is how to make the transition. Let me share a few ideas that may help you.

1. Develop respect for your destiny.

Respect the destiny you have birthed. Expect it to succeed. Today, I sit in my home office writing while many different things are being accomplished by the church I lead. Missions efforts are being funded and engaged around the world. New life groups are being planned. Back to school survival packets are being created for teachers in our local school department. There are people praying for the weekend services. Preparations are happening for baptisms. These are just a few things that I know are going on right now.

You are not separate from your destiny. You are playing your part and trusting that it can handle the rest.

In this moment, I'm not personally engaged with any of those efforts and I expect every one of them to succeed. Why? Because I respect the God-designed destiny I'm part of. My destiny is bigger than me, and I've learned to live within my destiny.

Respecting your destiny means trusting its ability to handle itself. Let's be clear. You are not separate from your destiny. You are playing your part and trusting that it can handle the rest.

For a business owner, this may mean handing off responsibilities to others. A parent may need to trust their grown child to make good decisions. A writer may need to allow another version of their creation to be offered. A leader might be challenged to trust those they lead to follow his or her vision. Whatever it looks like in your life, respect for your destiny will allow you to transition, but lacking respect will cause you to retain total control or walk away.

2. Let destiny define you, not consume you.

Vision and purpose empower you through the process, but their powerful effects can consume you. You were created to deliver the destiny and letting go becomes difficult. Through this book, I've given examples of both business people and church leaders who were birthing something great, but could not give it the space to grow. This results in misery for the bearer and an underperforming destiny. I'm thankful that Mary allowed Jesus to leave the house and begin doing what He was called to do.

> *A destiny is all-encompassing, but it should not be all consuming.*

A destiny is all-encompassing, but it should not be all consuming. For years, Kristy and I were unhealthy because birthing our destiny consumed all the resources we had to give. Earlier, I shared that we were holding two Sunday services and a Wednesday service. I was also teaching seventeen personal Bible Studies per week in individual homes. I was working like crazy, but after two years, a congregation of about twenty-five people and our marriage were both falling apart. I was consumed with bringing forth a destiny and forgetting to be a husband and father. I was reaching for more and being a poor steward of what was I already had. Unless something changed, I was going to lose it all.

I have no doubt of what my destiny is. I am designed to impact the world by developing the local church, but that is not all that I am. I'm also a husband, father, son, brother, and friend. My destiny becomes part of me, but it cannot be all of me. I am a leader in the same moment I am everything else.

A mother cannot stop being a woman, wife, daughter, sister, employer, or employee simply because she has a baby. Life doesn't work that way. While motherhood is always a part of her, it's not all that she is. In time, her children will grow up and move out of the house, and she will continue to be everything she ever was.

Your destiny will only flourish if it has the space to grow. Mary will forever be defined by her baby, but she also lived outside of what that baby meant. After scripture tells of the life and death of Jesus, we don't read much about Mary, but her life continued. While some traditions teach that Mary never had other children, scripture seems to indicate that she did.[55] My intention is not to debate a teaching point, but to show that Mary's life continued after Jesus stepped into His full authority. Her life didn't end with the realization of Jesus.

Being consumed by your destiny sounds like a good idea until it grows beyond you and you cease to exist. If Mary managed to survive, you can too!

3. Expect your destiny to outlive you.

Kristy and I have always agreed on one point while raising our children: our job was to shape them into viable adults not just happy children. While we obviously wanted them to experience happiness, their momentary happiness was not the driving force behind our parenting. The difference may be subtle, but it is certain to us. We were raising children into adults who would outlive us. We know we will not be around to help them for the rest of their lives. If they didn't learn how to deal with life's problems while they were small, they would be crushed when the problems became big.

This played out beautifully one afternoon in Tyrian's life. Our family had been inside a convenience store for a few minutes. After getting back into the car and driving for a while, we discovered that Tyrian had filled his pockets with candy. We had walked out of the store without paying. Our youngest son was a thief!

Our response was to turn the car around and drive back to the store. I said, *"Tyrian, stealing is wrong. We are going to go into this store, give them back their candy, and you are going to apologize for stealing."* He was not happy. When we entered the store, tears were flowing from his big blue eyes. His hands shook as he placed the candy on the counter, and his voice was soft as he spoke through tears, *"I'm sorry I stole this candy."*

The clerk was a nice older woman who said, *"It's ok, baby."* She meant well, but I couldn't let the moment end with her consoling my tiny thief. I calmly replied, *"No, ma'am, it is not ok. You are ok with my five-year-old stealing this candy from your employer, but would you be so gracious to a twenty-five-year-old driving away in your car?"* She looked at me and said, *"No, I guess I wouldn't."*

A God-designed destiny will always outlive you. Don't settle for raising something that dies with you. Your destiny is too important to disappear.

I replied, *"I'm raising a man. He just looks like a little boy right now."* I'm proud to say that I don't worry about either of my boys' honesty today. They confess things to their mother and I that they know they could get away with. They confess because they are men. They know how to take responsibility for their actions.

The day will come when I leave this Earth, and I pray they are healthy and strong. I have great confidence that they are going to have successful lives because Kristy and I birthed destinies we expected to outlive us.

A God-designed destiny will always outlive you. Don't settle for raising something that dies with you. Your destiny is too important to disappear.

I have a great memory of touring the George Ranch in Richmond, Texas. This ranch has been run by one family for over one hundred years. Kristy and I were alone when we approached the blacksmith's shop where an older gentleman was using bellows to gently blow air onto the fire. He had just finished up a demonstration, but that group had moved on. He looked up to see Kristy and me and asked what we would like to see. I could see the many examples of what he could create displayed around the shop. It was impressive. His iron art wasn't what captured my curiosity, however. I wanted to know why he was creating them at all. It was almost one hundred degrees and humid. We were sweating just walking around, and this man was hunkered over a fire keeping it hot. I wanted to know why.

He explained, *"I don't make much money doing this. A friend of mine introduced me to smithing. It intrigued me to think that by learning how to do this, I'd be connecting back to people from hundreds of years ago. It is a beautiful skill that is dying out, but I think it's too important to let it die. That's why I'm here."* His passion was infectious.

It's possible to experience great fulfillment by giving life to something that moves beyond you.

He believes that this art form is too important to disappear. I believe that any God-designed destiny should outlive the generation that gave it life. If you can develop respect for your destiny, not allow it to consume you, and expect it to outlive you, then you will make a healthy transition. You will learn to live within your destiny rather than outside of it.

Depending on where you are in the process, this concept may be impossible to comprehend. The thought of letting go of the baby you are nurturing may fill you with a sense of dread. Let me encourage you with the following statement: Proper delivery of your destiny will bring peace to the transition.

It's possible to experience great fulfillment by giving life to something that moves beyond you. A few years after leaving Kona, I was having lunch with a younger pastor. He asked how the church in Hawaii was doing. I responded that it had grown substantially since we left. I was confused when he responded by saying, *"That must suck!"* I asked, *"What do you mean?"* He said, *"I don't imagine it feels good to have the church grow after you are gone. It's like you don't matter anymore."* I was dumbfounded.

I said, *"You have daughters. How would you like it if they stopped growing when you weren't there? Would you be ok if they died when you did? Do you want them to disappear if something happens to you? Or would you rather they continue to live and thrive even after you are gone?"* He sat for a moment then answered sheepishly, *"I guess I didn't think about it like that."*

I don't blame him. He is a good guy with a strong ministry and a great future. He was falling into a common destiny trap. He was giving himself more importance than his destiny. Eventually, a destiny's future becomes its own and the one who brought it into the world will look on with a smile. If approached properly, there can be peace in the transition.

Are you willing to live within your destiny or must you walk away? Walking away may feel good, and the idea of relinquishing all responsibility isn't all bad, but it usually means being unable to interact with what you bore. Living within your destiny gives you the opportunity to indefinitely interact with the fruit of your life. The rewards are enormous!

CHAPTER 26

Your Story Continues

Birthing a destiny from conception to realization is no small task. It takes vision, courage, and incredible strength. We have seen that it is a process of processes. I hope you have discovered that the process is worthwhile. I pray that you have recognized that your destiny encompasses more than a single delivery. Birthing your destiny is one of the most rewarding things you will ever do.

A young man once told me that it was his destiny to play music in front of thousands of people. I wondered, *"What happens after you do that for the first time. Does your destiny cease to exist? Are you suddenly without a destiny? Have you outlived your purpose?"* This young man was obviously not considering a single performance, but a lifetime of moving crowds through music. I wonder how many people have created a company, family, career, or invention and now feel empty. If that's how you feel, you may be asking, *"Am I done? Is my purpose finished?"* The answer is, *"No."* A purpose, a destiny, continues.

The destiny of Mary was to birth the Son of God. She agreed to the conception, managed the expectation, survived the delivery, navigated the realization, and her life was not over. By many standards it had just begun. At the time of Christ's birth, Mary would have been between twelve and fourteen years old. There was nothing odd about this. It was the common age for betrothal and marriage then. There is no doubt about Mary's destiny, but at fourteen years old, she was certainly not done living! She still had a great life before her. She gave birth to Jesus and went on to be a great wife to Joseph and mother to Joseph, James, Jude, and Simon.[56]

In the first chapter of this book I wrote, *"This book is for people to understand that there is a future designed for you. Just as Mary was called by God to fulfill a particular purpose, you are called by God for a particular purpose. There is something that God has specifically designed you for, a job to complete, a destiny to fulfill. It may not be the angel Gabriel who stands before you in your room. There may be no declaration as specific as Mary's. There will, however, be a moment when what God has called you to do will become clear. A moment when your mind will be captivated by a particular idea. That idea will float across your mind and crystalize, becoming sharper by the moment. It will be then that your spirit will respond. The idea may seem crazy, it may be entirely outside of what is normal or usual, but something about it calls to you, and it won't let you go. Your destiny is calling."*

Your specific destiny will become clear and will rarely involve a single delivery. Throughout the book, I've written about birthing a destiny that included a marriage relationship, sons, and a church. These things are all important, and any one of them could become the single focus of my existence, and they're all part of my overall God-designed destiny.

I know that my God-designed destiny is to impact the world through the development of the local church. That destiny includes being a husband and a father. Having a healthy marriage and strong family is beneficial to having a healthy ministry. In my life, the relationship between Kristy and I has empowered me to fully pursue the ministry purpose I'm created for. I would not be nearly as effective without her. I know God brought us together for His purpose. This means that neither our marriage nor our sons are competing destinies, vying with the development of a church. It means that each element delivered from my life is part of a single destiny. Each stage is given life in sequence.

A God-designed destiny will always be moving God's purpose forward. The business you birth can create a healthy working environment for many people, allowing others to use their gifts and support their families. The family you create could impact the world with Christ's message through the example you set, the friendships you make, and the futures you develop through your children. The music you write may change hearts by creating an inspiring environment with a positive message that impacts the listener deeply. No matter what it may look like in your life, your destiny will move God's purpose forward in your life and in the world. Every element of life will ultimately play a part in your destiny.

> *A God-designed destiny will always be moving God's purpose forward.*

While interviewing mothers for this book, I discovered a unique trend. Most women expressed a fondness for a particular part of the process. Some ladies said the closeness shared with their husbands during the process of conception was meaningful. While the process of conception played a part, they gained a greater meaning by knowing they were intentionally bringing a new life into the world. Other mothers said the time of expectation was especially rewarding. Feeling the weight of the child grow as it developed brought a sense of peace, and its movements were fulfilling. Surprisingly, a few ladies even expressed their connection to the delivery process. The act of pushing the child into the world caused pain, but also gave a rewarding sense of power. While some of the older mothers I've spoken with have expressed their pride in who their children have become, no one has identified the child moving out as their favorite part of the process.

Releasing your child into the world can leave you feeling empty and alone. You have just moved through the stages of conception, expectation, delivery, and realization. Your life has been focused on developing this child, and now they are operating without your assistance. It's everything you hoped for, but what we hope for isn't always enjoyed in the end. Some couples suffer from what is commonly known as *"empty nest syndrome."* Releasing your destiny can result in the feeling of emptiness, but that is not always the reality. Some couples celebrate the last child leaving the home and look forward to a new chapter of life. Either way, your story is not over!

The process of birthing a child is not easy and is often painful. The many pitfalls typically leave the bearer feeling exhausted. One must conclude that any family daring to have one child would never have a second, but that would be a false conclusion. Strangely, before their first child is even out of diapers, either the husband or wife will look at the other and say, *"Do you want to have another one?"*

Maybe you have moved through the process successfully. Your destiny is being realized, but somewhere deep within you is the knowledge that something is stirring. You recognize that even as you've watched with joy as your child has matured, a concept has begun to percolate. It's just something that has crossed your mind a time or two. It's nothing major, but you think it bears some closer examination. In fact, you may know someone who could be interested in exploring the possibilities it could offer. You recognize that feeling...and it's exhilarating.

If that's how you feel, this book is for you. I encourage you to dive back in, starting from page one...

<<<<>>>>

Notes

Chapter 1
1. Luke 1:28; New King James Version
2. Luke 1:38; New King James Version

Chapter 2
3. Acts 1:14
4. Genesis 1:26; New Living Translation
5. Genesis 1:26; New Living Translation

PART 1

Chapter 3
6. Macworld from IDG; https://www.macworld.co.uk/feature/apple/history-of-apple-steve-jobs-mac-3606104/
7. Galatians 4:4; New Living Translation
8. Genesis 1:28; New Living Translation
9. Genesis 4:1; New Living Translation
10. Luke 6:45; New Living Translation
11. 2 Corinthians 5:7; New Living Translation
12. Matthew 1:20; New Living Translation

Chapter 4
13. Luke 1:35; New Living Translation

Chapter 5
14. Legacy Church is now New Hope Legacy. It is a thriving nondenominational church in Kona, Hawaii. It began as an independent church and is now part of the New Hope International Fellowship.
15. Ephesians 5:21
16. Matthew 16:18; Colossians 1:18
17. Ephesians 5:25; New King James Version
18. Luke 1:38; New Living Translation

Chapter 6
19. Galatians 4:4; New Living Translation
20. Micah 5:2; New Living Translation

21. Nazareth was between 80 and 108 miles from Bethlehem depending on which route was traveled.

Chapter 7

22. Leah's story is found in Genesis chapter 29

23. Genesis 29:32; New Living Translation

PART 2

Chapter 9

24. Woman's Health Magazine; March 25, 2015; A Doctor Explains How A Woman Can Go Nine Months Without Knowing She Is Pregnant; https://www.womenshealthmag.com/mom/didnt-know-i-was-pregnant

25. Luke 2:5 & 6; New Living Translation

26. James 2:26; New Living Translation

Chapter 10

27. Merck Manual Consumer Version; http://www.merckmanuals.com/home/women-s-health-issues/normal-pregnancy/stages-of-development-of-the-fetus

Chapter 11

28. Paraphrase of John 21:3

29. What Got You Here Won't Get You There: How Successful People Become Even More Successful; Marshall Goldsmith
30. Matthew 3:19; English Standard Version

Chapter 12

31. Isaiah 28:11-12; Matthew 11:28-29

32. Luke 2:6; New Living Translation

Chapter 13

33. Luke 2:6; New Living Translation

PART 3

Chapter 15

34. http://www.businessinsider.com/startup-failures-2011-5

35. Luke 2:6-7; New Living Translation

36. http://www.dailymail.co.uk/health/article-2112656/Woman-lie-upside-75-DAYS-save-lives-premature-children.html
37. Revelation 13:8

38. Hebrews 12:2; New King James Version